Scriptural Allusions in the New Testament

The Dead Sea Scrolls &
Christian Origins Library
5

Scriptural Allusions in the New Testament

Light from the Dead Sea Scrolls

by
Dale C. Allison, Jr.

BIBAL Press
North Richland Hills, Texas

BIBAL Press
An imprint of D. & F. Scott Publishing, Inc.
P.O. Box 821653
N. Richland Hills, TX 76182
817 788-2280
www.dfscott.com

Printed in the United States of America

04 03 02 01 00   5 4 3 2 1

Library of Congress Cataloging-in-Publication Data
Allison, Dale C.
  Scriptural allusions in the New Testament : light from the Dead Sea
scrolls / Dale C. Allison, Jr.
    p. cm. -- (The Dead Sea scrolls & Christian origins library ; 5)
Includes bibliographical references.
  ISBN 0-941037-78-9 (trade paper : alk. paper)
  1. Dead Sea scrolls--Criticism, interpretation, etc. 2. Bible.
N.T.--Criticism, interpretation, etc. 3. Dead Sea scrolls--Comparative
studies. 4. Bible. N.T.--Comparative studies. 5. Bible.
O.T.--Criticism, interpretation, etc., Jewish. 6. Dead Sea
scrolls--Relation to the New Testament. I. Title. II. Series.
  BM487 .A784 2000
  225.6--dc21
                          00-012024

All images copyright © 2000 by www.arttoday.com
Book design by Brenda Rodriguez & April McKay

Contents

Foreword
An Echo Thrown Back From a Hollow

S peech and language are possible only because of memory. As with a fugue in music, so a sound in speech is shaped by the echoes of the preceding one and defines the sense of the following one.

Words take on meaning only in a context; they can obtain new meaning with a different context. Change in meaning may occur, for example, with the addition of an adjective (that is, altering the context); hence, "" means someone is hurt, but "fatal *injury*" means that the person is not injured but dead. Th*injury*is example is also an oxymoron far more stunning than "cold hotdog," which makes sense only to one who knows, and probably has eaten, a warm hotdog. Only in a dictionary and phonebook do we find words and nouns separated from each other on the page; there is neither author nor an appeal to memory. Only idiots read dictionaries or phonebooks out loud to themselves at night. One who might hear such "readings" would recognize sounds but no meaning.

With poetry, human speech is elevated to somatic music; and memory is even more essential in poetry than in prose. The ancient Hebrew poets well knew that fact. They constructed their creative thoughts through repetitions. For example, they repeated sounds (assonance), movement (meter, rhythm and rhyme), basic units of meaning (paronomasia), and parallel thoughts. The highest form of poetry was to present a thought in two (or three) parallel lines. The memory of what had been said added to the next thought, and then to the total conception. Note these examples (translation is according to *TANAKH*):

The people that walked in darkness
Have seen a brilliant light;
On those who dwelt in a land of gloom
Light has dawned. [Isa 9:1]

"I have made a covenant with My chosen one;
I have sworn to My servant David:
I will establish your offspring forever,
I will confirm your throne for all generations." [Ps 89:4]

Attentive readers, who ponder and reread the lines reflectively, learn from Isa 9:1 that the "people that walked in darkness" have also "dwelt in a land of gloom." These people have already "seen a brilliant light," and that is because "Light has dawned." Readers can comprehend from Ps 89:4 that the covenant with David is also with his "offspring forever," and that is because God's "chosen one" is none other than "David." The important function played by memory in such Hebrew poetry is rightly called *parallelismus membrorum*, paralleled compositions that spring to life with meaning because of memory.

Sometimes a spoken word is followed by silence. Then language is complete, because the end is reached. The final unutterable syllable explains that the flow of thought is over, and reflection on the whole may now begin. That is when language becomes a pellucid window to wisdom. And, let us never forget, that language resides foremost in silence; otherwise we hear merely noise and bedlam.

Great literature consists of intermittent echoes of great thoughts. Authors add depth and symbolism to their creative compositions by noting expressions hopefully memorized by the intended reader. Once, memory was not drowned out by the intrusive noise of today (like musak). Once, the well-educated were learned in the humanities. Then, texts–sacred and profane—were memorized. And poetry known by heart helped add subtle depths to human utterance.

The Dead Sea Scrolls can be seen as scripture reshaped for new needs. The Jews who used scripture in these Scrolls helped shape human reflection. Their art was writing which rose to eloquence through the memorized Torah. Fortunately, the scripture of these authors has become the scripture of Jews and Christians today. Hence the Dead Sea Scrolls resonate with echoes of scripture.

The noun "echo" appears only three times in the Revised Standard Version of the Bible; each time it is only in the apocryphal books

(Wis 17:19, 3 Macc 1:29, Wis 18:10). One will not find the word "echo" in the Hebrew Bible (Old Testament) or in the Dead Sea Scrolls, because the noun does not exist in Hebrew. It is a Greek loan word in English in which it is merely transliterated (Gk. *ēcheō*).

The New Testament books themselves sometimes seem like echoes of older scripture. A key to such allusions is provided by the intertextuality of the old in the new at Qumran; that is, the men of the Dead Sea Scrolls spoke Biblical Hebrew. Their compositions were scripture *redivivus*. Professor Allison, whom long ago was taught to read the ancient scripts of the Qumranites, has listened to the voices of Qumran. He explains in the following pages how scriptural echoes reverberate in the Dead Sea Scrolls, and moreover, how their way of interpreting scripture clarifies and enriches our understanding of many traditions attributed to Jesus by the authors of the New Testament. He has opened our eyes and ears to many subtle nuances often missed until one stops, listens, ponders, and remembers the older text embedded or echoing in a new text. The result is a refined appreciation of the genius of the evangelists.

If we wish to understand more fully our sacred texts, we must keep an eye open for possible subtexts that echo in the text. The subtexts in the background of the text can become like rays of light that clarify a vague symbolic language. This language has been nurtured within a community that receives life from texts and then shapes those texts and creates other new ones.

From the very first page, Allison recovers some allusions and echoes that had been lost. He begins with an illustration taken from Martin Luther King's most famous speech. King eloquently used allusion, alluding to Lincoln, Shakespeare, Amos, Isaiah, the old hymn "America" and–of course—Moses' vision of the Promised Land he would not be able to enter. Allison shows how biblical allusions, or echoes, in the New Testament obtain new meaning when one sees how such allusions are interpreted in the Dead Sea Scrolls; for example, Zechariah's apocalypse in CD 19 (in his seventh chapter). Allison is correct to claim that the Bible uses words "that point beyond themselves"; that is, the biblical books "are literature of inheritance, being deliberately interactive and full of allusive reciprocal discourse" (p. 4). I find Allison's book both fascinating and enlightening.

When we first went to the mountains as children, we all learned that echoes are frequently not easily heard; they are more silent than the original sounds. One needs to pause, listen attentively, then ponder and reflect. Echoes in literature are just like that; pausing, listening, pondering why Martin Luther King used certain words, we eventually hear more than his own words. We hear the words of Moses and the sound of an enslaved people rising up to freedom.

Some echoes may never be heard and may be too obscure for us. For example, I doubt that many heard the echo in the title of this note. It begins in the *Wisdom of Solomon*, when the Jewish author describes the lawless men who held power over the holy nation and were paralyzed with terror, by "an echo thrown back from a hollow of the mountains" (WisSol 17:19).

J. H. Charlesworth
George L. Collord Professor of New
    Testament Language and Literature
Director of the Princeton Dead Sea
    Scrolls Project
Princeton Theological Seminary

Introduction

In his speech of 1968 at the Memphis Mason Temple, the Reverend Martin Luther King Jr. said that he had "been to the mountaintop" and had "seen the promised land." He also stated, prophetically, "I may not get there with you." These words do not name Moses. But who would deny the allusion to the lawgiver? King was implicitly likening himself to Moses' experience of looking across the Jordan River and being told he could not enter the promised land. In doing so, King was characterizing himself as well as the circumstances of his audience. He could have dully declared, "I have seen a better day, although it may be further off than hoped." He preferred, however, to create implicit yet crystal clear allusions to a shared world of religious ideas; he thereby cast upon his words an added dimension not soon forgotten. By evoking the rich tradition that likens the experience of African Americans to the experience of Israel in Egypt, King summoned the ghosts of a sacred history and made his speech more memorable and more forceful. Allusions can have such power.

King was adept at enlarging the meaning of his words through inexplicit borrowing from the past. His famous "I Have a Dream" speech is full of meaningful borrowing. It opens, for instance, with "Five score years ago," a manifest allusion to Abraham Lincoln's first words in his "Gettysburg Address" ("Four score and seven years ago . . ."). Several examples of inexplicit borrowing follow:

> ➤ "This sweltering summer of the Negro's discontent" echoes "Now is the winter of our discontent made glorious summer by the son of York" from Shakespeare's *Richard III*.
> ➤ "We will not be satisfied until justice rolls down like waters and righteousness like a mighty stream" draws upon Amos 5:24.

1

> ➤ "Every valley shall be exalted, every hill and mountain shall be made low, the rough places shall be made plain, and the crooked places shall be made straight and the glory of the Lord will be revealed and all flesh shall see it together" is from Isa 40:4–5.

> ➤ "We hold these truth to be self-evident, that all men are created equal" is a quotation from the Declaration of Independence.

> ➤ "So let freedom ring from the prodigious hilltops of New Hampshire. Let freedom ring from the mighty mountains of New York, etc." takes up the language of the old hymn, "America."

King's borrowing from and allusions to traditional texts constitute more than simple ornamentation. The use of Lincoln implies that King's cause is the continuation or completion of the freeing of the slaves. The allusion to Shakespeare is a way of asserting that King cannot be easily dismissed—he is intimately familiar with the educational tradition of his white opponents. The lines from the Bible make appeal to a sacred text with authority for both the white and African American communities and, more than that, imply that God is on King's side. The use of the "Declaration of Independence" and "America" announce that King is a patriot—some had slandered him for not being such—whose dream for his people in particular is the fulfillment of the American dream in general.

What we find in so many of King's speeches, namely, the expansion of meaning through inexplicit borrowing and allusion, is a common rhetorical feature of traditional Jewish and Christian literature, whether ancient, medieval, or modern. To the recent examples from King, I should like to add another, this from one of Protestantism's most famous old hymns, Augustus Montague Toplady's "Rock of Ages" (1776).

> Rock of Ages, cleft for me,
> Let me hide myself in Thee!
> Let the water and the blood,
> From Thy riven side which flowed,
> Be of sin the double cure,
> Cleanse me from its guilt and power . . .

These lines are helpful because they show us how dense allusions can be. Toplady's first four lines allude to or draw upon at least four scriptural texts, and some of the words have more than one referent. The dominant image is of water and blood flowing from

Christ's riven side to undo the guilt and power of sin. John 19:34 is clearly being alluded to: "one of the soldiers pierced his side with a spear, and at once blood and water came out." But the image of a dead Christ on the cross is not alone; it has rather been conflated with the image of water coming out of the wilderness rock that Moses struck (see Exodus 17; Numbers 20). And that is not all, for Christ is directly addressed as the rock that was cleft, and that presupposes the identification in 1 Cor 10:4: "and the rock was Christ." Finally, in lines 1 and 2, plain use has also been made of Exodus 33, where Moses hides in the cleft of a rock while the glory of the Lord passes by. The allusions then may be set forth like this:

"Rock" (= Christ)	1 Cor 10:4
"Rock" + "cleft" + "hide"	Exod 33:22
"Rock" + "water" + "flowed"	Exodus 17; Numbers 20
"water" + "thy riven side" + "flowed"	John 19:34

Whether or not contemporary singers of "Rock of Ages" perceive all these allusions, many eighteenth century Protestants, having grown up hearing the Bible read every evening, probably did. And I believe that their performance in this particular hymn may be likened to the performance of many ancient Jews and Christians: through religious education, which included the oral performances of Scripture in religious services, they knew their traditions sufficiently well to hear the biblical books as many of them were intended to be heard, as a collection of allusions.

Almost every book in the Hebrew Bible and New Testament is charged with allusion. From at least the Babylonian exile on, Jewish literary history—this includes the New Testament—is to a significant degree a chain of responses to foundational traditions (especially those preserved in the Pentateuch). The biblical books are typically designed to move their readers back to "subtexts." So in order to appreciate those books fully one must see behind them, to the texts in the background. Without such vision, interpretation is constricted—just as it would be for a hearer of King's speech who did not know Lincoln, Shakespeare, or the Bible. Meaning would remain, but it would be a shallow, surface meaning.

Another way of putting this is to say that much of the Bible is fundamentally elliptical. It says much in few words, in words that point beyond themselves, for the canonical writings are literature of inheritance, being deliberately interactive and full of allusive reciprocal discourse. Paul, for example, was adept at the traditional rhetoric of allusion as well as of citation. Not only did the apostle sometimes expect his readers to recognize a citation from the Hebrew Scriptures even when it had no introductory formula (as in Rom 10:13; 11:34–35; and 12:20), but his letters contain numerous allusions to Scripture. Moreover, as recent work has persuasively shown, often his arguments seem to assume an audience that can pick up those allusions and draw out implicit meaning. But Paul was hardly the only Christian of whom this may be said.

Consider an example from the Gospel of Mark. Mark 6:30–44 recounts the feeding of the five thousand. In this we run across the anomalous remark that the grass upon which the crowd sat was "green." The remark is anomalous because Mark's Gospel is almost devoid of what might be called novelistic details. We are never told what Jesus looked like, what Capernaum looked like, what Peter's boat looked like, or what the Jerusalem Temple looked like. In chapter 15, it is true, Roman soldiers dress Jesus in a "purple" cloak. Here, however, the color is mentioned in order to make plain that the clothing is an item of mocking: the alleged "king of the Jews" is being made up like a king. Otherwise, however, Mark's Gospel is colorless. So one must ask, why bother to note that the grass was green?

The likely answer is that there is a subtext beneath the feeding of the five thousand. Mark tells us that the crowd is like a sheep without a shepherd before Jesus takes care of them, supplying their want. The setting is near the seashore in the evening. And the grass is green. Surely the informed reader is to pick up echoes of the 23rd Psalm: "The Lord is my shepherd, I shall not want. He makes me lie down in green pastures. He leads me beside the still waters." The picture in both texts is the same: the shepherd cares for his flock as they lie down on the green grass by the water, and the sheep have no lack.

Many modern readers may consider this sort of allusion to be rather subtle. But this is largely because we live in a time of verbal inflation, of throwaway utterances. The sheer volume of verbiage produced by our society, for paper and for wave transmission, has reduced the value of words so that we now need more to say less. The result is that we are not so accustomed to the phenomenon of few words signifying much. But we should not allow our historically conditioned deafness to blind us to oblique allusions in the Bible.

A contemporary analogy may encourage us, the more so as ancient "readers" were in fact always "listeners." Those who habitually listen to music over the radio can often identify a popular song after hearing just the smallest portion of it. There are in fact contests that require people to name a musical piece after hearing only a slight excerpt from it, one lasting no more than a second or two, and consisting of no more than two or three notes or cords. The uninitiated will discern only noise. But to those with the requisite musical knowledge (gained, be it noted, not through arduous study but through effortless listening), the briefest extract can conjure up a world—a song, an album, a musical group. It appears to have been similar with those Jews who wrote the Dead Sea Scrolls (hereafter DSS) and the Christians who wrote the New Testament. We are sometimes forced to pick up a concordance in order to perceive connections that were once immediately grasped by the conditioned ears of their audiences with unconscious sureness.

Once, however, we see that the Bible is a bit like poetry, that much of its power is the power of suggestion, that it often hints rather than says, or that it so to speak says more than it says, we face a problem. The Roman poet Ovid says that he imitated his predecessor Virgil not to steal but in order to borrow openly, with the intention of being recognized (Seneca the Elder, *Suasoriae* 3.7). But how does the contemporary reader of an ancient work recognize such intention? When is an allusion an allusion? We may believe that we are reading books that are incomplete utterances and full of holes, that we must make present what is absent, that we must become actively engaged and bring to a text knowledge of what it presupposes. But how do we figure out exactly what it presupposes? We can always use the exegetical talents we have to discover animal shapes in clouds. Diligent searching can always unearth resemblances between two texts—most of them comparatively meaningless. Of the drawing of many parallels there is no end. The mind can always connect two things in an infinite number of ways. How then do we sort out the meaningful? Again, when is an allusion an allusion?

Anyone familiar with the critical literature on the New Testament knows that the hunting of allusions is an uncertain enterprise. Surely John 1:51 ("you will see heaven opened, and the angels of God ascending and descending upon the Son of Man") has something to do with Jacob's ladder and Gen 28:12. But does Mark 10:45 ("to give his life as a ransom for many") draw upon Isaiah 53? And is Rom 8:32 (God "did not spare his own Son but gave him up for us all") a reminiscence of Genesis 22 and the offering up by Abraham of his son Isaac? The texts are silent and scholars disagree. How then does one decide? All concur that the New Testament books, not unlike "The Waste Land" of T. S. Eliot, constantly elicit tradition through the device of allusion. But whereas Eliot condescended to footnote his famous poem, the New Testament writers did not add footnotes or commentary. As modern readers of the Bible we are in the same position as the college student struggling to understand Dante or Milton in an old edition, one without extensive notes. Every phrase has something in it, much more than initially perceived, but how do we perceive it? Time removes us from all texts and subtexts (as well as from their earlier interpretations) and so cripples our ability to detect tacit references—which is why, as history marches on, annotated editions of the classics become longer and longer. The exoteric always, with time, becomes the esoteric. How many twentieth-century readers of Milton's famous XVIth Sonnet would, unaided, grasp the meaning of "that one talent which is death to hide" (the allusion is to Matt 25:14–30, the parable of the talents)? Commentary is now required. With age, transparent allusions become delicate cross-references that are now the discoveries of the learned.

I cannot, in a book of this scope, spend any time trying to establish exactly how we may gain confidence that we are reading out of a text rather than into it. And in any case there is in the end no simple answer. Only a delicate and mature judgment bred of familiarity with a tradition will be able to feel whether a suggested allusion is solid or insubstantial. The truth must be divined, groped for by taste and experience rather than some sort of scientific method.

It is the purpose of this little book, however, to show the reader that the Dead Sea Scrolls are of great help in this difficult task. Not only does the richly allusive scriptural combinations in a text such as *11QMelchizedek* confirm that Jewish writers were well-versed in the same sort of rhetorical skill King excelled in, but— and this is what this book is all about—they assist us in another way. For they sometimes confirm our belief that a particular subtext lies beneath a particular New Testament text. In chapter 2, for instance, we shall see that many have found in the dove at Jesus' baptism an echo of Gen 1:2 and the creation story. This interpretation is now strongly supported by the Dead Sea Scrolls, in which we find an application of Gen 1:2 strikingly similar to that posited for Mark. Again, in chapter 5 we shall see that the proposal that 2 Samuel 7 is one of the subtexts behind the scene of Jesus' trial in Mark 14 is much more plausible now that we know what the Dead Sea Scrolls do with 2 Samuel 7. In other words, by showing us how certain biblical texts were understood and used, the Scrolls help us better comprehend how certain scriptural allusions function in the New Testament.

Before turning to the texts, however, I should like to raise briefly the question: What is the difference between a citation and an allusion? Why does the New Testament sometimes cite and sometimes allude?

It has recently been observed that, if modern scholars are correct, Paul's habit was not to cite confessional or liturgical formulas (cf. 1 Cor 15:3–4) but rather to allude to them. Such formulas belonged to the special language of the Christian communities, they were the language of insiders. So the use of such language allusively was one way of binding people together. Sharing a particular idiom that outsiders do not understand gives people something very important in common and so helps cement their communal bonds. Allusive language can be a way of drawing group boundaries and reinforcing feelings of group membership.

But there is another aspect to be underlined. The functions of formal citation and of allusion are different. The former typically calls attention to itself for the purpose of adding authority. This explains the pattern of scriptural quotations in the authentic Pauline epistles. There are no formal citations at all in Philippians, Colossians, 1 Thessalonians, 2 Thessalonians, or Philemon. And whereas the Corinthian correspondences average less than one formal citation per chapter (14 + 7 citations for 16 + 13 chapters), the six chapters of Galatians contain ten such citations, and Romans, with its sixteen chapters, has forty-eight. The explanation for these distributions is that Paul tended to quote Scripture explicitly in polemical situations in which his opponents were also citing Scripture. When writing to the Romans and Galatians, the apostle needed the traditional court of appeal, the authoritative Scriptures.

The primary purpose of allusions, however, is not to add authority or help clinch arguments. Their general effect is instead to stimulate readers to become more active. In any context, the explicit soon becomes tedious, and the allusion is a way of fighting tedium. Meaning is infolded not to obscure but to improve communication: allusions give the imagination more to do and so heighten attention. The implicit allows the pleasure of discovery, and readers who are invited to fill gaps appreciate authors who respect them enough not to shout. The reader who is invited to do more work is the more appreciative.

A simple illustration of how all this works appears in the book of Wisdom. Chapter 10 summarizes the stories of great individuals from Adam to Moses—without once mentioning anyone's name. Adam is "the first-formed father" (10:1). Cain is "an unrighteous man" (10:3). Noah and Abraham and Lot and Jacob and Joseph are all called "a/the righteous man" (10:4, 5, 6, 9, 13). Moses is "a servant of the Lord" (10:15). Clearly the author of Wisdom intentionally avoided naming his subjects. And just as clearly he expected his readers to do this simple thing for themselves. Why? The silence draws readers further into the book by asking them to make their own contribution. Perhaps, too, the absence of names is an enticement to turn the unnamed into types or symbols. For this, allusions are just what are needed—more would be less.

Matters were, I should like to suggest, similar with the texts to be examined in this book. Like the readers of Wisdom 10, early Christians, alive to the biblical texts they had read or heard again and again, filled in the implicit blanks in their texts. Hearing this or that suggestive phrase, or the right combination of words, they would quickly recall a subtext. That is, their informed imaginations were encouraged by allusions to Scripture to explore all sorts of potential meaning. For whereas the quotation makes for closure, the allusion, like the parable and the apocalyptic symbol, opens up possibilities for the informed imagination. It expands the horizon of potential understanding. It evokes. How this sometimes happened we will now see.

The Dove at the Baptism and Gen 1:2

According to Matt 3:16; Mark 1:10; and Luke 3:22, when Jesus was baptized in the river Jordan, the Spirit of God descended upon him. Mark puts it this way: "When he [Jesus] came up out of the water, immediately he saw the heavens opened and the Spirit descending upon him like a dove." Whether the concluding expression, "like a dove" (the Greek is, ὡς περιστερὰn), qualifies "Spirit" and so means that we are to envisage the Spirit as having the form of a dove, or whether the words are adverbial and refer instead to the manner of the Spirit's descent, is unclear, and the commentaries disagree. The commentaries likewise differ on the significance that "like a dove," within either reading, should be given. Few any longer assume that we have here the simple record of a historical fact. That is, that "like a dove" appears in the gospels because, as a matter of historical experience, Jesus or others actually saw something that reminded them of a dove. Rather, "like a dove" probably had for the first readers a symbolic significance or a theological implication. In other words, we are here dealing with someone's *interpretation* of Jesus' baptism. But what exactly was being conveyed?

Several possibilities suggest themselves. Some scholars, observing that 1 Pet 3:20–21 compares the deliverance of Noah to baptism, have maintained that the reader should recall the dove that Noah sent out according to Gen 8:8–12. When Noah released his dove, it was to determine whether the waters had subsided from the earth, to determine whether the time of judgment had passed. So perhaps some early Christian added the dove to the story of Jesus' baptism in order to express the conviction that the advent of Jesus closed a time of judgment and ushered in a new era of salvation: the kingdom of God had arrived.

A second possible interpretation holds that we have a motif from folklore. In fairy tales throughout the world there are texts in which the true king is shown to be such by the selection of a bird. That such a motif could have had a place in early Christianity is proven by its appearance in the second-century *Protevangelium of James*. This tells the apocryphal tale of a how a husband was picked for the Virgin Mary. The story has it that Zacharias was instructed by an angel to have the widowers of the people assemble to the Temple with rods. They did so with Joseph among them. Then the high priest took the rods into the Temple, prayed over them, and returned them to the widowers—whereupon a dove flew out of Joseph's rod and lighted upon his head, proof enough that God had chosen him to wed Mary. In like manner, could not the dove of the Synoptics be a sign that God chose Jesus?

Yet a third possible interpretation of Mark 1:10 and its parallels observes that Israel is portrayed as a dove in Hos 7:ll and other extra-biblical sources. So perhaps one should think of Jesus' emergence from the waters as the emergence of renewed Israel. One recalls that there is a passage in the *Mekilta*, an early rabbinic commentary on Exodus, which claims that, at the crossing of the Red Sea, the Holy Spirit rested upon Israel, and that Israel was then like a dove.

Despite all that may be said in favor of the three interpretations just introduced, probably a majority of modern commentators have preferred to look to Gen 1:2 as the most obvious source for elucidation of the dove. This verse declares that, at the creation of the world, "The Spirit of God was hovering over the face of the waters." We have here three elements that reappear in the baptism story: the Spirit of God, water, and the image of a bird. (One may compare Deut 32:11, where the verb translated as "hover" in Genesis is plainly applied to a bird).

Favoring this proposal is a passage in the Babylonian Talmud, in *b. Ḥag.* 15a. In this the hovering of God's Spirit at the creation is likened explicitly to the hovering of a dove:

> Our Rabbis taught: Once R. Joshua b. Hanania was standing on a step on the Temple Mount, and Ben Zoma saw him and did not stand up before him. So [R. Joshua] said to him: Whence

and whither, Ben Zoma? He replied: I was gazing between the upper and lower waters, and there is only a bare three fingers' [breadth] between them, for it is said: And the Spirit of God hovered over the face of the waters—like a dove which hovers over her young without touching [them].

What would have been the point of likening the baptism of Jesus to what happened when the world began? The answer is obvious. Early Christians, drawing upon the eschatological expectations of Judaism, imagined the better world of the future as a return to the beginning: the end would be paradise regained. "The last things [will be] like the first," to quote the second-century *Epistle of Barnabas*. This is why Rev 22:1–5 depicts the future as a return to Eden. Just as God, in the beginning, created a paradise with a tree of life in it (Gen 2:9; 3:22, 24), so too will the divinity create a second paradise with another tree of life (Rev 22:2). And just as God, in the beginning, set a river in Eden (Gen 2:10), so too will a river be set in the new Jerusalem of a new earth (Rev 22:1). Furthermore—and this is my main point—because early Christians thought of Jesus as bringing the eschatological renewal, they often likened his advent and its consequences to the creation of the world. Consider just three New Testament texts:

> "The first man, Adam, became a living being; the last Adam became a life-giving spirit" (1 Cor 5:45)

> "If anyone is in Christ, there is a new creation; everything old has passed away; see, everything has become new!" (2 Cor 5:17)

> "He [Jesus] is the image of the invisible God, the firstborn of all creation; for in him all things in heaven and on earth were created . . . He is the beginning, the firstborn from the dead . . ." (Col 1:15–21)

In the light of passages such as these, very near to hand is the thought that the descent of the dove at Jesus' baptism, designed to trigger memories of Gen 1:2, signified to readers steeped in Jewish Scripture and tradition that Jesus was the bringer of a new creation. If at the commencement of things the Spirit of God hovered over the face of the watery chaos, at the Messiah's advent the Spirit fluttered over the waters of the Jordan. In other words, when Jesus came into the world a new age commenced, and God, through the Holy Spirit, renewed the great work of creation.

With this tentative conclusion in mind, we may turn to an important Dead Sea Scroll fragment that was first published in 1991, in the *Biblical Archaeology Review* [vol.17, no. 6: p. 65.]. The fragment is now known as "4QMessianic Apocalypse," or *4Q521*. The text, which foretells, in its two readable columns, the wonderful messianic future, when the heavens and the earth will obey the Messiah, is important and fascinating for a number of reasons. For one thing, there is the clear reference to *one* Messiah (other scrolls seem to refer to two Messiahs). For another, there is heavy borrowing from passages in Isaiah, a borrowing that, as we shall see in another chapter, irresistibly reminds one of the string of Isaianic allusions in Matt 11:2–6 and Luke 7:18–23. Here is what remains of fragment 2, column 2:

> [1] [for the heav]ens and the earth will obey his Messiah, [2] [and all] that is in them will not turn away from the holy precepts. [3] Be encouraged, you who are seeking the Lord in his service! [4] Will you not, perhaps, encounter the Lord in it, all those who hope in their heart? [5] For the Lord will observe the devout, and call the just by name, [6] and upon the poor he will place his spirit, and the faithful he will renew with his strength. [7] For he will honour the devout upon the throne of eternal royalty, [8] freeing prisoners, giving sight to the blind, straightening out the twisted. [9] Ever shall I cling to those who hope. In his mercy he will jud[ge,] [10] and from no-one shall the fruit [of] good [deeds] be delayed, [11] and the Lord will perform marvelous acts such as have not existed, just as he sa[id] [12] for he will heal the badly wounded and will make the dead live, he will proclaim good news to the meek [13] give lavishly [to the need]y, lead the exiled and enrich the hungry. [14] [. . .] and all [. . .].

For our immediate purposes, which have to do with understanding the baptism of Jesus, attention needs to be directed to the sixth line: "upon the poor he will place his spirit." The Hebrew of the first half of the line is this: ועל ענוים רוחו תרחף. This is a clear allusion to Gen 1:2: "and the Spirit (רוח) of God was hovering (מרחפת) over (על) the face of the waters." It would seem that the author of our scroll, when contemplating the eschatological redemption, moved his thoughts back to Genesis 1, to the story of creation. That is, he appropriated the language of Gen 1:2 to characterize the eschatological redemption: just as the Spirit of God once hovered over the face of the waters, so too, at the end, will the Spirit hover over the saints and strengthen them.

4Q521 falls into the same category as the New Testament texts cited above, the texts that see the latter days as a return to the beginning. So in this respect the New Testament is following pre-Christian Jewish theology. This is something we already knew from Jewish texts such as Isa 65:17 ("For I am about to create new heavens and a new earth") and 4 Ezra 7:30 (at the end "the world will be turned into the primeval silence seven days, like as at the first beginnings"). But now we know more. With the publication of *4Q521* we know that this theological idea is the correct one for interpreting the dove at the baptism.

Before the newly released fragment, the interpretation of the dove in terms of Gen 1:2 could not cite any specific Jewish precedent. There were plenty of Jewish texts that transferred creation imagery to the consummation, but no pre-Christian instance of the application of Gen 1:2 in particular to the eschatological future. Furthermore, there was no clear example of the image of the Spirit hovering over human beings as opposed to hovering over lifeless material, as in Gen 1:2 (there over watery chaos). Once more, however, the new fragment makes up the lack: it foresees the Spirit of God hovering over the poor, that is, the saints. It follows then that those who have understood the baptismal dove to function as an allusion to Gen 1:2 have had their judgment much strengthened, indeed all but confirmed. We now have clear precedent for the creative application of the language of Gen 1:2 to eschatological matters and precedent for picturing the Spirit as hovering over people.

The previous paragraph assumes that *4Q521* is Jewish, not Christian. Two or three few scholars have wondered whether it might not be the latter. The majority of scroll scholars, however, think otherwise, and they seem to be right. The text itself is in no particular way explicitly Christian. More importantly, in the judgment of nearly all the experts, no other Dead Sea Scroll has yet been shown to have been composed by followers of Jesus.

Even if, however, one were to hold that the new text is Christian, the interpretive implications would be pretty much the same. We would still have new first-century evidence for a creative application of Gen 1:2 that coincides in significant respects with what many modern commentators have found in Mark 1:10; Matt 3:16; and Luke 3:22.

The New Moses of
the New Exodus

t the beginning of the Sermon on the Mount, we read that
Jesus, upon seeing the crowds, went up on a mountain and
there sat down in order to teach his disciples (Matt 5:1–2). It has
been common throughout exegetical history to think of Matthew's
mountain as a counterpart to Sinai. In the words of Matthew Henry,
"Christ preached this sermon, which is an exposition of the law,
upon a mountain, because upon a mountain the law was given." Not
only does Matthew's Greek recall pentateuchal passages having to
do with Moses (e.g. Exod 19:3, 12, 13), but Jewish tradition spoke of
Moses *sitting* on Sinai (so already a pre-Christian work known as the
Exagogue of Ezekiel). Furthermore, other Moses typologies from
antiquity have their Mosaic heroes sit on a mountain (for example,
the one in the fourteenth chapter of the apocalypse called *4 Ezra*);
and Matt 8:1, the conclusion of the Sermon on the Mount, is identi-
cal with one Greek version of Exod 34:29 (LXX A), which recounts
Moses' descent from Sinai. This means that the Jesus of the Sermon
on the Mount is designed to remind us of Moses.

This is confirmed by what has come earlier in the Gospel.
Indeed, an extensive Moses typology runs throughout Matthew's
first few chapters. The story of Joseph's contemplation of what to
do about Mary, suspected of adultery, and of the angel who bids
him not to fear and then prophesies his son's future greatness (see
chapter 1), parallels the story of Amram, Moses' father, as told by
Josephus, in *Antiquities* 2:210–16: Amram, ill at ease over what to
do about his wife's pregnancy, has a dream in which God exhorts
him not to despair and then prophesies his son's future greatness.
Matthew's "You are to name him Jesus, for he will save his people

from their sins" (1:21) reminds one, moreover, of Moses' status as "savior" of his people (Josephus, *Antiquities* 2:228; *b. Sota* 12b).

In chapter 2, Herod's order to do away with the male infants of Bethlehem (2:16–18) is like Pharaoh's order to do away with every male Hebrew child (Exodus 1). Similarly, just as Herod orders the slaughter of Hebrew infants because he has learned of the birth of Israel's liberator (2:2–18), in Jewish tradition Pharaoh slaughters the Hebrew children because he has learned of the very same thing (Josephus, *Antiquities* 2:205–209; *Targum of Pseudo-Jonathan* on Exod 1:15). Further, whereas Herod hears of the coming liberator from chief priests, scribes, and magi (2:1–12), Josephus, in his *Antiquities* 2:205 and 234, has Pharaoh learn of Israel's deliverer from scribes, while the *Jerusalem Targum* on Exod 1:15 says that Pharaoh's chief magicians (Jannes and Jambres, the sons of Balaam) were the sources of his information. The quotation of Hos 11:1 in Matt 2:15 further evokes thought of the exodus, for in its original context "Out of Egypt I have called my son" concerns Israel. And then there is 2:19–2, which borrows the language of Exod 4:19–20: just as Moses, after being told to go back to Egypt because all those seeking his life have died, takes his wife and children and returns to the land of his birth, so too with Jesus: Joseph, after being told to go back to Israel because all those seeking the life of his son have died, takes his wife and child and returns to the land of his son's birth.

In chapter 3, Jesus is baptized by John the Baptist. We know from 1 Cor 10:1–5 that baptism could be likened to passing through the Red Sea. In chapter 4, commentators have long associated Jesus' forty days of fasting with Moses' forty days of fasting, as well as with Israel's forty years of wandering and being tempted in the wilderness. In line with this, when the devil takes Jesus to a very high mountain to show him all the kingdoms of the world (4:8), one may think of Moses seeing across the Jordan from the top of Pisgah, for, among other things, not only does Matt 4:8 use the language of the Greek version of Deut 34:1, 4, but Jewish tradition expanded Moses' vision so that he beheld all of the world.

The apparent allusions to Moses and the exodus in Matthew 1–5 appear in their biblical sequence:

slaughter of Jewish infants
return of Israel's deliverer
passage through water
temptation in wilderness
commandments from mountain

This is not the upshot of chance. Given his status as one like Moses, it is no surprise at all that Jesus, when he goes up on a mountain, exhorts his hearers about murder, adultery, divorce, oaths, revenge, and love. These are all topics that Moses addresses in Deuteronomy, and Jesus in fact more than once quotes Moses himself regarding them (see Matt 5:21–48). So Jesus is like the law-giver in this regard too.

This sort of extended comparison between a hero and Moses in Matthew can be found elsewhere in Jewish literature. Already the book of Joshua sets its hero beside Moses. In Josh 1:5 the Lord says to Joshua: "As I was with Moses, so I will be with you;" and in 1:17 the Reubenites, the Gadites, and the half-tribe of Manasseh declare to their new leader: "Just as we obeyed Moses in all things, so we will obey you." This setting of Joshua beside Moses in chapter 1 prepares for chapters 3–4, where Israel, under Joshua's command, crosses the Jordan River—a miracle that puts us in mind of Moses leading the children of Israel through the Red Sea. After the Jordan is crossed we are told: "on that day the Lord exalted Joshua in the sight of all Israel; and they stood in awe of him, as they had stood in awe of Moses" (4:14). There is also this: "The Lord dried up the waters of the Jordan for you until you passed over, as the Lord your God did to the Red Sea, which he dried up for us until we passed over" (4:23).

From the duplicating pattern that runs throughout much of Joshua the scripturally literate reader infers that the God of the exodus is also the God of the promised land. One might make a similar point with regard to Matthew's Moses typology: the God of Jesus is the God of Moses. Although there is much truth to this reading, there is more than this within Matthew's comparison.

Matthew's Moses typology is not confined to the first few chapters. It appears several times thereafter. One place in which it plainly occurs is in Matthew's version of Jesus' transfiguration, 17:1–9. "Six days later" (17:1, an anomalous chronological specification, but see

Exod 24:16) Jesus' face shines like the sun (17:2) as does Moses' face in Exod 34:29–35. As in Exod 24:15–18 and 34:5, a bright cloud appears, and a voice speaks from it (cf. Exod 24:16). The onlookers—a special group of three (17:1; compare Exod 24:1)—are afraid (17:6; compare Exod 34:29–30). And all this takes place on a mountain (17:1; compare Exod 24:12, 15–18; 34:3). Moreover, Moses and Elijah, who converse with the transfigured Jesus, are the only figures in the OT who speak with God on the Mountain called sometimes Sinai and other times Horeb, so their presence together makes us think of that mountain.

Now, special note should be taken of what the divine voice from the cloud says. It says, "This is my beloved son, hear him." Many commentators have found in this declaration an echo of Deut 18:15 and 18. The former reads, "The Lord your God will raise up for you a prophet like me [Moses] from among you, from your brethren—*him you shall hear.*" The latter reads, "I [God] will raise up for them a prophet like you from among their brethren; and I will put my words in his mouth, and he shall speak to them all that I command him." The suggestion is that the voice at the transfiguration is informing us that Jesus is like Moses precisely because he is the prophet like Moses to whom Israel should listen.

Perhaps most Hebrew Bible scholars think that the original meaning of the prophetic words in Deuteronomy was that God would from time to time raise up a prophet like Moses; that is, here a whole series of prophets or even something like a prophetic institution is envisaged. We know, however, that early Christians understood the words differently. For them they were not a forecast of Joshua and other prophets later on. Rather they were a forecast of Jesus. In Acts 3, Peter says, among other things, the following:

> And now, friends, I know that you acted in ignorance, as did also your rulers. In this way God fulfilled what he had foretold through all the prophets, that his Messiah would suffer. Repent, therefore, and turn to God so that your sins may be wiped out, so that times of refreshing may come from the presence of the Lord, and that he may send the Messiah appointed for you, that is, Jesus, who must remain in heaven until the time of universal restoration that God announced long ago through his holy prophets. Moses said, "The Lord your God will raise up for you from your own people a prophet like me. You must listen to

whatever he tells you. And it will be that everyone who does not
listen to that prophet will be utterly rooted out of the people."

This passage claims that Jesus the Messiah is the prophet envisaged by Moses in Deuteronomy 18. The same contention is implicit in John 6. Here people, after the miracle of the loaves, which
is compared with the miracle of Moses and the manna, exclaim,
"This is truly *the* prophet who is coming into the world." The definite article ("the") betrays the fact that here a definite figure is in
view. Given that Jesus is here a prophet and has just done something very much like Moses, one again thinks of Deuteronomy 18:
Jesus is being made out to be the prophet like Moses.

Scholars have debated the extent to which the expectation of
a prophet like Moses who would come at the end of days was
known among first-century Jews. The belief is missing from the
rabbinic corpus, and there are only uncertain testimonies to it in
Philo, in the Apocrypha, and in the Pseudepigrapha. The Dead
Sea Scrolls, however, now reveal to us that Christians were not the
only ones who thought of an end-time prophet when they read
Deut 18:15 and 18.

In the so-called *Rule of the Community*, in *1QS* 9:9–11, we find
this: "They [the members of the Qumran community] should not
depart from any counsel of the law in order to walk in complete
stubbornness of their heart, but instead shall be ruled by the first
directives which the men of the community began to be taught, until
the prophet comes, and the anointed ones of Aaron and Israel."
This text looks into the future, to the time when God will set things
right once and for all, and it foresees God sending three eschatological figures—a priestly Messiah (the anointed one of Aaron), a
Davidic Messiah (the anointed one of Israel), and "the prophet."

The identity of this last is clarified for us in another document
known as *Testimonia* (*4QTestim*). It cites Deut 18:18–19 (see above),
Num 24:15–17 (the oracle of Balaam which speaks of a star from
Jacob and a scepter from Israel), and Deut 33:8–11 (this concerns
the authority of Levi the high priest). Now the passage from Deuteronomy 33 is intended to ground in Scripture the expectation of
a Levitical Messiah while the passage from Numbers is a proof text
for the expectation of a Davidic Messiah. What then of the quotation from Deuteronomy 18? Obviously it is intended to show that
Scripture foretells the coming of an eschatological prophet who

will be like Moses. In other words, if *1QS* 9:9–11 prophesies the coming of the prophet, the priestly Messiah, and the Davidic Messiah, *Testimonia* supplies us with three proofs texts, one for each of those figures. The proof text for the prophet like Moses is Deut 18:18–19, which is the text that lies behind the New Testament claim that Jesus is "the prophet who is coming into the world" (John 6:14). This is the prophet Moses predicted would be like him (Acts 3:22–23), the one people should heed (Matt 17:5).

If Christians claimed that Jesus fulfilled the prophecy of Deut 18:15 and 18, a prophecy that, in its original context, is not at all obviously about an eschatological figure, the Dead Sea Scrolls now show us that those verses were understood by some pre-Christian Jews to foretell an eschatological prophet.

But the Scrolls may offer even more in this connection. Quite a few scholars have supposed that the Righteous Teacher, a formative figure in the sect's history about which we unfortunately know all too little, was identified with the eschatological prophet of Deuteronomy 18, or that he was at least reckoned a sort of second Moses.

One possibility is that *1QS* 9:11 (quoted above) is from a portion of the *Rule of the Community* that was composed before the advent of the Righteous Teacher, and that the sect saw in the Teacher the prophet who would come at the end of the age. There are good arguments that suggest portions of *1QS* 8 – 9 represent the earliest literary stage of the document and indeed reflect the ideology of a sect before the establishment at Qumran. So it is quite possible that a pre-Qumran group expected a righteous teacher according to an eschatological interpretation of Deut 18:15 and 18, and that subsequently one arose who was held to fulfill that expectation.

There is in any case no denying a certain resemblance between the Righteous Teacher and Moses. The former, leader of a desert community that had experienced a new exodus, was a teacher and interpreter of the law. He was "raised up" (*CD* 1:6), just as Deut 18:15, 18 and *4Q175* foretell that God will "raise up" the prophet like Moses (in each case the Hebrew verb is the same, קום). The Righteous Teacher was also known as the "faithful shepherd" (*1Q34* bis ii 8), a title the rabbis gave to Moses, and he was believed to be a prophet at the end of days, who spoke from "the mouth of God" (*1QpHab* 2:2–3; compare Numbers 12:6–8) who had come to guide a people who were theretofore wandering "in a pathless wilderness" (*CD* 1:15). He had a special understanding, greater than the writing prophets themselves (*1QpHab* 2:9; 7:3–5). He was an object of faith, as was Moses (*lQpHab* 2:7–8), and people were to listen to him (*1QpHab* 2:7–9; *CD* 20:28–34; compare Deut 18:15–18).

One may further observe that the Righteous Teacher is given the title "vessel" (*CD* 6:7–8) just as is Moses in the targums and rabbinic texts. Of even more interest is *1QH* 12(4):5 ("You have illumined my face with your covenant"; compare 12[4]:27–29). There are good reasons for assigning this part of *1QH* to the Righteous Teacher himself. This matters because the author of *1QH* 12(4):5 – 13(5):4 may well have been likening himself to Moses. The hymnist's *face* has been illumined by God's covenant, as is Moses' face in Exodus 24 and 34. God has appeared to him (12[4]:6; compare Exodus 33). He is the mediator of the law, which is written on his heart (12[4]:10). And the faithful "listen" to him (12[4]:24; compare Deut 18:15, 18).

The evidence is enough to allow us to claim that the sect behind the Dead Sea Scrolls saw in its leader someone like Moses—and that, like the early church, it looked for and recorded parallels between the two men. It is also just possible that, more specifically, some saw in the Righteous Teacher the fulfillment of Deut 18:15, 18, the prophecy that God will raise up a prophet like Moses. If so, we have a striking parallel to what happened with the early Christians.

The one difference, however, would be that whereas Christians identified the prophet like Moses with Jesus the Messiah, the Qumran sect thought of the prophet like Moses as separate from the Messiah. Whether that is because some pre-Christian Jews, like the rabbis but unlike the authors of the Scrolls, already thought of the Davidic Messiah as being Mosaic the extant sources do not allow us to say.

The Baptism of Christ
(drawing of a detail from the cathedral at Ravenna, Italy)

John the Baptist
A. Ivanov

Nathan before David
(late 19th-century illustration)

David
(bust by Michelangelo)

Left:
Isaiah (frieze by
Michelangelo)

Below:
Artist's concep-
tion of Solomon's
Temple (Donne P.

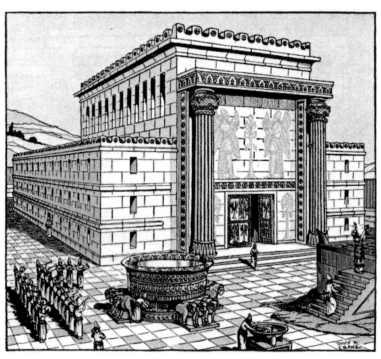

Left:
19th-century
engraving of
Sermon on
the Mount

20th-century illustration of Moses coming down from

Above: Christ Entering Jerusalem, Fra Angelico

Below: Early 20th century illustration,
Jesus before the Sanhedrin

The Transfiguration, Raphael

Pentecost, El Greco

Excommunication and Lev 19:17–18

Matt 18:15–20 contains the following ecclesiastical regulation:

> If another member of the church sins against you, go and point out the fault when the two of you are alone. If the member listens to you, you have regained that one. But if you are not listened to, take one or two others along with you, so that every word may be confirmed by the evidence of two or three witnesses. If the member refuses to listen to them, tell it to the church; and if the offender refuses to listen even to the church, let such a one be to you as a Gentile and a tax collector. Truly I tell you, whatever you bind on earth will be bound in heaven, and whatever you loose on earth will be loosed in heaven. Again, truly I say to you, if two of you agree on earth about anything you ask, it will be done for you by my Father in heaven. For where two or three are gathered in my name, I am there among them.

This paragraph, which has a distant parallel in Luke 17:3, is intriguing for several reasons. The first one is exegetical. How should these instructions be related to Matt 7:1–5, where disciples are told that they are not to judge others? How can one who is prohibited from judging others follow the procedure outlined in Matt 18:15–20?

A second reason this text garners so much interest is that it has been used in controversial ways down through the ages. Some have cited it as a support for the authority of church councils. As Pope Leo (*Epistle* 98:1) put it, if Christ is present with two or three, how much more a whole company of bishops! But those supporting the government of the Free Churches have also called upon our text: Christ is present for any two or three gathered in his name; no institution is required. Still others have invoked Christ's promise to be present when two or three are gathered together against Christian solitaries, such as monks, nuns, and ascetics who have chosen to live by themselves. For example, according to the long recension of Ignatius, *Letter to the Ephesians* 5, "If the prayer of one or two possesses such power that Christ stands in their midst, how much more will the prayer of the bishop and the whole church, ascending up in harmony to God, prevail for the granting of all their petitions in Christ. So those that separate themselves from such and do not meet in the society where sacrifices are offered . . . are a wolf in sheep's clothing." An old papyrus, on the other hand, seems to contain a rejection of this way of thinking about Matt 18:20: "Where there are three, they are without God, and where there is but a single one, I say that I am with him" (*P. Oxyrynchus* 1:23–27).

A third reason Matt 18:15–20 generates so much interest is because of the intriguing parallels in Jewish texts. "For where two or three are gathered in my name, I am there among them" recalls a saying attributed to Rabbi Hananiah ben Teradion in the Mishnah: "But if two sit together and words of the Torah are between them, the divine presence rests between them" (*ʾAbot* 3:2). Similar is the saying attributed to Rabbi Simeon ben Yohai in *ʾAbot* 3.3: "If three have eaten at one table and have spoken over it words of Torah, it is as if they had eaten from the table of God."

It is possible that the saying of Rabbi Haninah was called forth by the gospel saying as a kind of counterblast. More probably, however, it expresses what was a rabbinic commonplace—so that Matt 18:20 is a Christian revision of a rabbinic sentiment, in which Jesus replaces the Shekinah, or divine presence.

There is yet another striking parallel to Matt 18:20 in *ʾAbot*: "If ten men sit together and occupy themselves with in the Law, the divine presence rests among them, for it is written, God stands in the congregation of God. And when do we learn this even of five? Because it is written, And has founded his group upon the earth. And whence even of three? Because it is written, He judges among the judges. And when even of two? Because it is written, Then they that feared the Lord spoke one with another, and the Lord hearkened and heard. And whence even of one? Because it is written, In every place where I record my name I will come unto you and I will bless you" (3:6; the same tradition appears also in the *Mekilta* on Exod 20.24). Again, although one might conjecture that the rabbinic text was prompted by the saying preserved in Matthew, it seems more likely that this and the other rabbinic texts cited above are independent of Christianity, and that Matt 18:20 is a Christian reformulation of a common rabbinic sentiment. Jesus, the fullness of God's glory (as in Heb 1:3; compare John 1:14), has simply been substituted for the Shekinah, the divine glory or presence, and the gathering together "in my name" for the study of Torah. As in the Mishnah, so in Matthew: the zone of the sacred is not dictated by geography but is mobile. The difference is that holy space is, so to speak, "Christified" in the gospel. It is entered into by gathering in Christ's name.

If the final sentence of Matt 18:15–20 has parallels in Jewish sources, the same is true for the first sentence, the command to reprove or point out another's fault, and to do this in secret. Consider these texts:

> Prov 3:12: "For the Lord reproves the one he loves, even as a father the son in whom he delights."

> Prov 25:9–10: "Argue your case with your neighbor directly, and do not disclose another's secret; or else someone who hears you will bring shame upon you, and your ill repute will have no end."

> Prov 27:5–6: "Better is open rebuke than hidden love. Well meant are the wounds a friend inflicts, but profuse are the kisses of a enemy."

> Sir 20:2: "How much better it is to rebuke than to fume."

These four texts are from the Hebrew Bible and the Apocrypha. Even closer is a passage from the *Testaments of the Twelve Patriarchs*, a pseudepigraphon that purports to pass on the dying words of the twelve sons of Israel. In one part of this work, which is often thought by scholars to be a Jewish production of the first-century, we find this:

> Now, my children, each of you love his brother. Drive hatred out of your hearts. Love one another in deed and word and inward thoughts. For when I stood before my father I would speak peaceably about Joseph, but when I went out, the spirit of hatred darkened my mind and aroused my soul to kill him. Love one another from the heart, therefore, and if anyone sins against you, speak to him in peace. Expel the venom of hatred, and do not harbor deceit in your heart. If anyone confesses and repents, forgive him. If anyone denies his guilt, do not be contentious with him, otherwise he may starting cursing, and you

would be sinning doubly. In a dispute do not let an outsider hear your secrets, since out of hatred for you he may become your enemy, and commit a great sin against you (*T. Gad* 6:1–5).

These words are very close to those attributed to Jesus in Matt 18:15–20. Indeed, it is a reasonable inference that the two texts are both developments of a common Jewish tradition, especially when one takes into account what the Dead Sea Scrolls have to say on the subject of reproof.

Before, however, taking up that matter, the scriptural background of *T. Gad* 6:1–5 needs to be considered, for there is an unmistakable subtext. Beneath *T. Gad* 6:1–5 lies the famous Lev 19:17–18: "You shall not hate in your heart anyone of your kin; you shall reprove your neighbor, or you will incur guilt yourself. You shall not take vengeance or bear a grudge against any of your people, but you shall love your neighbor as yourself: I am the Lord." Here we find the four imperatives of *T. Gad* 6:1–5—love your brother, do no hate him, reprove him if necessary, and forgive him. *T. Gad* 6:1–5 is not exactly an interpretation of Lev 19:17–18, but it does clearly offer a clarifying application of those words.

We find the same thing in the Dead Sea Scrolls, although here the issue is plainly discipline within the sectarian community, so that here we are even nearer to Matt 18:15–20. 1QS 5:24 – 5:2 has this:

> Each should reproach his fellow in truth, in meekness and in compassionate love for the man. No-one should speak to his brother in anger or muttering, or with a hard [neck or with passionate] spiteful intent and he should not detest him [in the stubbornness] of his heart, but instead reproach him that day so as not to incur a sin for his fault. And in addition, no one should raise a matter against his fellow in front of the Many unless it is with reproof in the presence of witnesses. In this way shall they behave in all their places of residence.

Here again the dependence upon Lev 19:17–18 is undeniable ("reproach his fellow," "compassionate love for the man," "reproach him," "so as not to incur a sin for his fault"). No less interesting for our purposes is the mention of witnesses from the community, which is a very large step towards what we find in Matthew's instructions of reproof.

There is a second text from the Dead Sea Scrolls that reviews the procedure for excommunication. Here Lev 19:17 and 18 are cited explicitly. *CD* 9:2–8 has this:

> And what it says: "Do not avenge yourself or bear resentment against the sons of your people": everyone of those who entered the covenant who brings an accusation against his fellow, unless it is with reproach before witnesses, or who brings it when he is angry, or he tells it to his elders so that they despise him, he is "the one who avenges himself and bears resentments." Is it not perhaps written that only "he (God) avenges himself and bears resentment against his enemies"? If he kept silent about him from one day to the other, or accused him of a capital offense, he has witnessed against himself, for he did not fulfil the commandment of God which tells him: "You shall reproach your fellow so as not to incur sin because of him."

Evidently the community at Qumran interpreted the imperative, "you shall reprove your neighbor, or you will incur guilt yourself" (Lev 19:17), to mean that if you see another commit some sin, it is your duty, in order to avoid guilt, to reprove that person. The reproof is to be undertaken in the presence of witnesses. But if that fails, the matter must be taken up before "the Many," that is, the elders or some official body of the community.

We may now return finally to Matt 18:15–18. Obviously behind it lies a Jewish tradition of rebuke based upon Lev 19:17–18. This important fact is bound to escape the modern reader, who will miss the allusion to that famous pentateuchal text. But Matthew's ancient Jewish audience no doubt knew the text from Leviticus well enough (it is quoted in Matthew no less than three times: 5:43; 19:19; 22:39). And so when they heard Jesus say that one is to "rebuke" (the Greek imperative is ἔλεγξον; in the Greek of Lev 19:17 it is ἐλέγξεις) a fellow disciple, they would no doubt have understood what was involved: Jesus was applying a commandment of Moses or rather turning it into a rule for church discipline.

This fact is full of hermeneutical relevance. For when Matthew's passage is read in the light of Lev 19:17–18, one cannot separate it from the commandment to love. In Leviticus, the necessity for rebuke is immediately preceded by the order not to hate and immediately followed by the imperative to love one's neighbor as oneself. It follows, with this in mind, that the hard and regrettable task of reproof and church discipline outlined in Matthew 18 must be undertaken in charity. There can be no self-interest, much less vengeance. Reproof, when necessary, will be for the sake of the sinner—this is why rebuke begins in private and only becomes public if there is no repentance.

That Matthew indeed felt all this deeply is manifest from the way he put together chapter 18. The teaching on excommunication is prefaced by 18:1–14, a collection of materials that demand humility (verses 1–5), the elimination of all stumbling blocks (verses 6–9), and exceptional kindness to all (verses 10–14). Matt 18:15–20 is then followed by Jesus' teaching on unlimited forgiveness (verses 21–22) and by a parable which reminds us that the failure to forgive is a failure to act as the heavenly Father acts (verses 23–35). Obviously Matthew has done his best to surround the difficult teaching on censure with sayings that constitute a hedge against rigidity and absolutism. Reproof must be an act of love or it is not in the spirit of Matthew.

One final observation about Matt 18:15–20 needs to be made. Lev 19:17–18 is not the only scriptural text upon which it stands. Informed readers should recall another pentateuchal passage, this one from Deuteronomy. "But if you are not listened to, take one or two others along with you, so that every word may be confirmed by the evidence of two or three witnesses" echoes Deut 19:15: "A single witness shall not suffice to convict a person of any crime or wrongdoing in connection with any offense that may be committed. Only on the evidence of two or three witnesses shall a charge be sustained." This Hebrew Bible verse was an important part of Jewish law (see for example *11QTemple* 61:6–7; 64:8–9). Early Christians, however, appear to have commonly applied it to church discipline. In addition to Matt 18:15–20, we find Deut 19:15 alluded to in 2 Cor 13:1, where Paul tells the Corinthians that any charges they make against one another "must be sustained by the evidence of two or three witnesses." And in 1 Tim 5:19 there is this: "Never accept any accusation against an elder except on the evidence of two or three witnesses." Once again, then, Matthew appears to stand within a tradition. That is, Matt 18:15–20 not only takes up a Jewish tradition based upon Lev 19:17–18, it also is in harmony with the application of Deut 19:15 found in 2 Cor 13:1 and 1 Tim 5:19.

The Trial of the Son of David and 2 Samuel 7

Mark 14:53–65 recounts the interview of Jesus before a hostile Sanhedrin. The passage bristles with difficulties and has generated a host of questions. What is its historical basis? How could Christians have discovered any information since none of them were witnesses? Did the Jewish authorities have the authority to execute criminals or not? How could they have met at night when rabbinic legislation prohibits such? Did Jesus really speak of himself as the Son of Man coming with the clouds of heaven, and if so what could he have meant?

All of these questions are legitimate and fascinating, but in this chapter I wish to explore another issue. This has to do with the logic of the narrative as it stands. There is for the careful modern reader a certain incongruity. Mark tells us that the chief priests and the whole counsel sought testimony against Jesus so that they might put him to death. They evidently had trouble finding it. We are told that at the last, however, "false witnesses" came forward with this accusation: "We heard him say, 'I will destroy this Temple that is made with hands, and in three days I will build another, not made with hands" (14:58). After obtaining this testimony, the high priest stands up and asks Jesus if he has no answer to make to the accusation. When Jesus is silent and makes no answer, the high priest in exasperation cries out, "Are you the Christ, the Son of the Blessed One?" (14:61).

At this point, the reader may want to know what has prompted this question. Nothing up to now has been said about Jesus being the Messiah or the Son of God. Why then the question about Jesus' identity as the Messiah or Son of God? It is as though the narrative

37

has jumped from one subject—Jesus as opponent of the Temple—to another—Jesus' claim to be the messianic Son of God.

One possibility is that there is in fact no connection between the two issues. Maybe we are to understand that since Jesus said nothing about the issue of the Temple, the high priest is forced to leave that problem aside and take up another in his attempt to catch Jesus out. Maybe the destruction and rebuilding of the Temple have nothing to do with Jesus' claims about himself.

But another solution commends itself. Already in Zech 6:12–13, we find this prophecy: "Here is a man whose name is Branch; for he shall branch out in his place, and he shall build the Temple of the Lord. It is he that shall build the Temple of the Lord; he shall bear royal honor, and shall sit upon his throne and rule. There shall be a priest by his throne, with peaceful understanding between the two of them." This is one of the texts behind the expectation, found in the Scrolls, of a Davidic Messiah and a priestly Messiah. But for our purposes, what matters is that this text from Zechariah would surely have been read, in Jesus' day, not as a fulfilled prophecy but as a promise yet to be fulfilled. Not only does the *Targum* on Zechariah—an Aramaic paraphrase of uncertain date—substitute "Messiah" for "Branch," but "Branch" is already a sort of title for the Davidic Messiah in the Dead Sea Scrolls (for example, *4QPatriarachal Blessings* 3 – 4: "Until the Messiah of Righteousness comes, the Branch of David . . .").

So Zech 6:12–13 raise the possibility of some sort of traditional connection between building the Temple and being Messiah. But there is another text that, even more than Zech 6:12–13, illuminates Mark's version of the trial of Jesus. This is 2 Sam 7:12–16, where the prophet Nathan speaks to king David with these words:

> When your days are fulfilled and you lie down with your ancestors, I will raise up your offspring after you, who shall come forth from your body, and I will establish his kingdom. He shall build a house for my name, and I will establish the throne of his kingdom forever. I will be a father to him, and he shall be a son to me. When he commits iniquity, I will punish him with a rod such as mortals use, with blows inflicted by human beings. But I will not take my steadfast love from him, as I took it from Saul, whom I put away from before you. Your house and your kingdom shall be made sure forever before me; your throne shall be established forever.

This prophecy is obviously about Solomon. He was David's son and built the Temple in Jerusalem. But ancient readers were not satisfied with leaving things at that. For the text promises that the kingdom of the son will be made sure forever; that is, his throne will be established evermore—and David's line eventually failed. So how could one make sense of Nathan's oracle?

The early Christians made sense of it by thinking of it as fulfilled in Jesus. The move was natural enough. Jesus was the Son of David. He was God's Son in a special sense. And he had spoken of raising up a new Temple, which Christians variously interpreted as his own resurrected body (so John 2:19–21) or the church (so probably Mark 14:58). The following verses, from three New Testament books, refer to Nathan's oracle and claim its fulfillment in Jesus:

> Luke 1:32–33: "He will be great, and will be called the Son of the Most High, and the Lord God will give to him the throne of his ancestor David. He will reign over the house of Jacob forever, and of his kingdom there will be no end."

> Acts 2:30: "Since he [David] was a prophet, he knew that God had sworn with an oath to him that he would put one of his descendants on his throne."

> Heb 1:5—"For to which of the angels did God ever say, 'You are my Son; today I have begotten you'? Or again, 'I will be his Father, and he will be my Son'?"

When we return now to Mark's trial narrative with all this in mind, things suddenly begin to clear. Jesus is accused of prophesying that he will destroy and rebuild the Temple. To this charge he maintains silence. But the high priest presses the issue and so asks Jesus if he claims to be the Messiah, the Son of God. The assumption is that if Jesus has really said that he will himself build the Temple, then he has made an implicit claim to be the eschatological fulfillment of Nathan's oracle, which foresees a descendant of David who will build the Temple, will be God's Son, and will rule in Israel. In other words, the question about Jesus' identity is not independent of the accusation about the Temple but follows directly from it. Once we recognize the subtext, Mark's narrative flows smoothly.

But we are left with one last question. Were the Christians the first to see in Nathan's oracle a prophecy of the Davidic Messiah of the last days, or had Judaism already come to read the prophecy this way? If the latter is the case, then one could still consider the possibility that Mark's narrative preserves historical memory when it joins Jesus' words about the Temple with the issue of Jesus' identity.

Before the Dead Sea Scrolls were discovered, we did not know the answer to the question. Jewish sources written after the New Testament show traces of an eschatological interpretation of 2 Samuel 14, but pre-Christian evidence was lacking. Not anymore—column 1 of fragments 1–3 of *4QFlorilegium* contains this:

> And as for what he [God] said to David, "I shall obtain for you rest from all your enemies: (it refers to this,) that he will obtain for them rest from all the sons of Belial, those who make them fall, to destr[oy them for their s]ins, when they come with the plans of Belial to make the s[ons of] light fall, and to plot against them wicked plans so that they are trapped by Belial in their guilty error. And Yahweh de[clares] to you that he will build you a house. I will raise up your seed after you and establish the throne of his kingdom [for ev]er. I will be a father to him and he will be a son to me." This (refers to the) "branch of David," who will arise with the Interpreter of the law who [will rise up] in Zi[on in] the last days, as it is written, "I will raise up the hut of David which has fallen" [Amos 9:11]. This (refers to) "the hut of David which has fallen," who will arise to save Israel . . .

These words clearly apply Nathan's oracle not to Solomon but to the messianic Son of David of the end times. God will raise up as a king the seed of David, and a house (= the Temple) will be built, and the Davidic kingdom will be established forever. In addition, the Davidic king will be God's son: "I will be a father to him and he will be a son to me."

We have here then a conflation of the themes in Mark 14:53–65. One must note, however, two differences. The first is that in *4QFlorilegium* it is God who builds the Temple, not the messianic Son of David. Although some scholars have made much of this difference, it really amounts to little because other Qumran texts can blur the distinction between divine and human action. The latter, after all, works through the former. This is why, in *4Q521*, God is the subject of the clause, "preach good news to the poor," but the unstated subject seems to be a messianic herald. Certainly the idea of God preaching good news in unmediated fashion is rather diffi-cult to envisage.

The second difference is that Mark refers not just to building but also to destroying. This has no counterpart in the Qumran materials. A parallel exists in *1 En.* 90:28, a pre-Christian text in which God removes the "old house" (= Jerusalem and its Temple) before establishing a "new house." This shows us it was possible to think of the old Temple being taken down and replaced by a new one. But equally important is the likelihood that Jesus himself, as a matter of fact, prophesied the destruction of the Temple, as all four gospels relate. That is, the formulation in Mark—destruction of temple, rebuilding of temple—derives not just from an exe-getical tradition or eschatological expectation of Judaism but from Jesus' own conviction that the Temple was about to pass away.

One final point should be made. The New Testament fre-quently calls Jesus "the Son of God." There has been much debate over the provenance of this title. One good possibility, consistent with the connection between 2 Samuel 7 and Jesus' confession in Mark 14, is that it owes something to Jewish messianic expecta-tion. We have already seen that *4QFlorilegium* applies Nathan's oracle, in which God says he will be a father to a descendant of David and that that descendant will be a son to him, to the eschato-logical Branch of David. This opens up the possibility that pre-Christian Judaism might already have sometimes thought of the Davidic messiah as God's son. The possibility is enhanced by an intriguing fragment from the Dead Sea Scrolls designated *4Q246*, which is often referred to as the *"Son of God" Text*, less often as *4QAramaic Apocalypse*. Its second column reads as follows:

> He will be called son of God, and they will call him son of the Most High. Like the sparks of a vision, so will their kingdom be; they will rule several years over the earth and crush everything; a people will crush another people, and a city another city. Until the people of God arises and makes everyone rest from the sword. His kingdom will be an eternal kingdom, and all his paths in truth and uprigh[tness]. The earth (will be) in truth and all will make peace. The sword will cease in the earth, and all the cities will pay him homage. He is a great God among the gods. He will make war with him; he will place the peoples in his hand and cast away everyone before him. His kingdom will be an eter-nal kingdom, and all the abysses . . .

Unfortunately the text, as said, is fragmentary, and this disallows a certain identification of the figure who is called "Son of God" and "Son of the Most High." Some have suggested he should be identified with an historical king of Israel, others with an Antichrist figure, still others that the Son of God is the angel, Michael, in his eschatological role. But many have instead given the text a messianic sense: the Son of God is the Messiah. The arguments in favor of this position cannot be marshaled here, but they should probably carry the day. One reason is the very close parallel in Luke: "He will be great, and will be called the Son of the Most High, and the Lord God will give to him the throne of his ancestor David. He will reign over the house of Jacob forever, and of his kingdom there will be no end" (1:32–33). This, as has often been observed, is strikingly close to *4Q246*, and it is a prophecy of the Messiah, Jesus. So while certainty eludes us, the Dead Sea Scrolls have given us additional reason to suspect that, among its other associations in a Jewish context, the title "Son of God" might very well have had royal messianic connotations, just as it seems to have in Mark's account of the trial of Jesus.

Uses of Isaiah in the Gospels and James

The book of Isaiah was as important to early Christians as it was to those who composed the Dead Sea Scrolls. Both groups saw in their own experience the fulfillment of oracles from the Hebrew Bible's largest prophetic book. It is no surprise, then, that in this chapter the Scrolls illumine several New Testament allusions to Isaiah. We shall focus on three.

Isaiah 5 and the Parable of the Wicked Tenants.

In Matt 21:33–44; Mark 12:1–11; and Luke 20:9–19 we find the so-called parable of the wicked tenants. Mark's version reads as follows:

> A man planted a vineyard, put a fence around it, dug a pit for the wine press, and built a watchtower; then he leased it to tenants and went to another country. When the season came, he sent a slave to the tenants to collect for them his share of the produce of the vineyard. But they seized him, and beat him, and sent him away empty-handed. And again he sent another slave to them; this one they beat over the head and insulted. Then he sent another, and that one they killed. And so it was with many others; some they beat, and others they killed. He had still one other, a beloved son. Finally he sent him to them, saying, "They will respect my son." But those tenants said to one another, "This is the heir; come, let us kill him, and the inheritance will be ours." So they seized him, killed him, and threw him out of the vineyard. What then will the owner of the vineyard do? He will come and destroy the tenants and give the vineyard to others . . .

Commentators have long noticed that Jesus' parable strongly resembles Isa 5:1–7:

> Let me sing for my beloved my love-song concerning his vineyard: My beloved had a vineyard on a very fertile hill. He dug it and cleared it of stones, and planted it with choice vines; he built a watchtower in the midst of it, and hewed out a wine vat in it; he expected it to yield grapes, but it yielded wild grapes. And now, inhabitants of Jerusalem and people of Judah, judge between me and my vineyard. What more was there to do for my vineyard that I have not done in it? When I expected it to yield grapes, why did it yield wild grapes? And now I will tell you what I will do to my vineyard. I will remove its hedge, and it shall be devoured; I will break down its wall, and it shall be trampled down. I will make it a waste; it shall not be pruned or hoed, and it shall be overgrown with briers and thorns; I will also command the clouds that they rain no rain upon it. For the vineyard of the Lord of hosts is the house of Israel, and the people of Judah are his pleasant planting; he expected justice, but saw bloodshed; righteousness, but heard a cry!

Both Jesus' parable and Isaiah 5 are about a vineyard and the divine judgment. But that here we actually have, beyond the similarity in theme, literary borrowing appears when we observe the similarities in the settings:

Mark	*Isaiah*
planting a vineyard	digging a trench
raising a fence	planting a vineyard
digging a winepress	building a tower
building a tower	digging a winepress

The Greek version of Isaiah 5 adds to these parallels, for there, as in the gospels but not the Hebrew text, we also read about raising a fence.

Before going further, we need to remark that Mark's parable is an allegory of sorts. This does not mean that all the details in it have symbolic meaning (although they have all been given such in exegetical history). It is rather that one can give equations for the main elements:

the vineyard stands for Israel
the householder stands for God
the tenant farmers stand for the Jewish leaders
the fruit stands for what is owed to God
the rejection of servants stands for the rejection of prophets
the sending of the son stands for the sending of Jesus
the rejection of the son stands for the rejection of Jesus
the punishment of the tenants stands for divine punishmen

Commentators have regularly made these equations. Unfortunately, they have also typically gone on to read our parable as a statement about the faithlessness and judgment of Israel as a whole and Israel's subsequent replacement by Gentiles who believe in Jesus. Our parable thus has long been understood as a statement of ethnic relations: the Jews rejected Jesus so God offered salvation to the Gentiles.

This interpretation gains some credence from the fact that, in Isaiah 5, the vineyard is equated with Israel (see above). There are, however, contradictory facts to be considered. For one thing, in the Synoptics the parable's context is not conflict between Jesus and Judaism but conflict between Jesus and the Jewish leadership of Jerusalem. For another, it is not the vineyard/Israel that suffers judgment, but the tenants in charge of the vineyard. Also, the parable identifies the tenants not with Israel in general but with Israel's leaders in particular. Mark is quite clear about this. After they hear the parable, "the chief priests, the scribes, and the elders" (Mark 11:27) perceive that the parable has been told against them. The crowds, on the other hand, are still on Jesus' side—"they [the leaders] wanted to arrest him, but they feared the crowd," Mark 12:12—so obviously they do not think that Jesus has condemned them.

Once we entertain the possibility that the traditional interpretation of Jesus' parable of the wicked tenants is incorrect, that the parable is less about Israel in its entirety than about a particular group within Israel, namely, the Jerusalem leaders in charge of the temple establishment, the allusions to Isaiah 5 take on new meaning. For the old *Targum*, or Aramaic paraphrase of Isaiah, differs from the Hebrew text in that it moves the focus of the parable from the Jewish people to the Temple: the vineyard is no longer the house of Israel (as in Isa 5:7) but Jerusalem and the Temple. The *Targum* renders Isa 5:2 this way: "And I sanctified them and I glorified them and I established them as the plant of a choice vine; and I built my sanctuary in their midst, and I even gave my altar to atone for their sins; I thought that they would do good deeds, but they made their deeds evil." For verse 5, the *Targum* then has this: "And now I will tell you what I am about to do to my people. I will take up my Shekinah from them, and they shall be for plundering; I will break down the place of their sanctuaries, and they will be for trampling." Here the divine judgment does not mean the end of God's relationship with Israel but the destruction of the Temple. (The *Targum* reflects the dreadful events of 70 CE, when the Romans invaded Judea and burned down the Temple.)

If we could be sure that Isaiah 5 was read as the *Targum* reads it already in the time of Jesus, we would have our clue as to why, according the evangelists, the Jerusalem authorities perceived that Jesus' parable in the vineyard was spoken against them. For the transparent allusions to Isaiah's parable, interpreted as a warning of judgment upon the Temple, would have constituted an indictment of the Jerusalem establishment. Unfortunately, however, it is very difficult to date any of the non-Qumran targums or the traditions enshrined in them. So we cannot simply cite the *Targum* on Isaiah 5 to settle our issue. Nor are we helped by the fact that the other rabbinic sources, such as *b. Sukk.* 49a ("'And planted it with the choicest vine' refers to the Temple"), agree with the interpretation in the targum. These sources are also too late for us to trust them as witnesses to the first century.

It is here that the Dead Sea Scrolls come to our assistance. Within them there is a poetic fragment that uses the language of Isaiah 5 and simultaneously refers to the Temple. That fragment is *4QBenediction* (*4Q500*). This blessing, presumably addressed to God, is short and full of gaps, but the following words can be made out:

> . . . may your baca trees blossom . . .
> . . . your wine vat built among stone . . .
> . . . at the gate of the holy height . . .
> . . . your planting and the streams of your glory . . .
> . . . the branches of your delights . . .
> . . . your vine[yard] . . .

The dependence upon Isaiah 5 is plain from the vocabulary. "Wine vat," "planting," "delights," and "vineyard" are drawn from Isaiah's parable. The vineyard, however, now appears to be on the temple mount.

The interesting fact for us about *4QBenediction* is that, despite its fragmentary nature, we can still see that it used the language of Isaiah 5 in connection with the Temple. For "the gate of the holy height" must refer to that structure. Furthermore, "the streams of your glory" is in all likelihood a reference to the channel that drained fluids from the sacrificial altar into the Kidron Brook (see *Yoma* 5:6). In the rabbinic source known as the *Tosefta*, in 3:15 of the tractate *Sukka*, Isaiah's "wine vat" is equated with the altar and that channel.

The implications of these facts about *4QBenediction* are far-reaching for the interpretation of Jesus' parable. We now know that there were pre-Christian Jews who found in Isa 5:2 a reference to the Temple. In other words, the interpretation in the *Targum* was known in New Testament times. This cannot but encourage those recent interpreters who have argued that Christian readers down through the centuries have probably read too much into Mark 12:1–12 when they have taken the passage to be about God's rejection of the Jews. Mark's editorial comment that it was precisely the Jewish leaders in Jerusalem who thought that the parable and its allusions to Isaiah 5 were directed against them in particular harmonizes with the more narrow interpretation of Isaiah found in the *Targum* and now the Dead Sea Scrolls. So the parable of the wicked tenants may be plausibly read as the record of a conflict between Jesus and the temple establishment, not as a testimony to God's rejection of the Jewish people.

Isa 40:2–9 and Jas 1:8–10.

Modern commentators typically observe that Jas 1:8–10 recalls Isa 40:6–8. The former reads in the NRSV: "Let the believer who is lowly boast in being raised up, and the rich in being brought low, because the rich will disappear like a flower in the field. For the sun rises with its scorching heat and withers the field; its flower falls, and its beauty perishes. It is the same with the rich; in the midst of a busy life, they will wither away." The latter reads: "A voice says, 'Cry out!' And I said, 'What shall I cry?' All people are grass, their constancy is like the flower of the field. The grass withers, the flower fades, when the breath of the Lord blows upon it; surely the people are grass. The grass withers, the flower fades; but the word of our God will stand forever."

The commentators generally leave the impression that we have here little more than an ornamental borrowing of scriptural language. But Jas 1:9–11 almost in its entirety reflects the language of Isa 40:2–9. One can see this at a glance:

Isa 40:2–9 (Greek version)	*Jas 1:9–11 (literal trans.)*
"Speak, priests, to the heart of Jerusalem. Comfort her, for her humiliation (*tapeinōsis*) is fulfilled, her sin is put away. For she has received double from the Lord's hand for her sins A voice of one crying in the wilderness, Prepare the way of the Lord, make straight the paths of our God. Every valley will be filled, and every mountain and hill will be brought low (*tapeinōthēsetai*) . . . A voice of one saying, Cry; and I said, What shall I cry? All flesh is grass (*chortos*), and all the glory of humanity is as the flower of the grass (*hōs anthos chortou*). The grass withers (*exēranthē ho chortos*) and the flowers falls (*kai to anthos exepesen*), but the word of our God abides forever. God up on a high (*hupsēlon*) mountain, O proclaimer of good tidings to Zion; lift up (*hupsōson*) your voice with strength . . . life it up (*hupsōsate*) . . .	Let the brother who is lowly (*tapeinos*) glory in his exaltation (*hupsei*), but the rich in his humiliation (*tapeinōsei*) because like a flower in the field (*hōs anthos chortou*) he will pass away. For the sun rises with the scorching wind and withers the grass (*exēranen ton chorton*) and its flower falls (*kai to anthos autou exepesen*), and the beauty of its appearance perishes. So also the rich in the midst of his pursuits will fade away.

The shared vocabulary is remarkable. Even one who does not know the Greek alphabet can see this at a glance:

Isa 40:2–4: ταπείνωσις . . . ταπεινωθήσεται
Jas 1:9–10: ταπεινός . . .   ταπεινώσει

Isa 40:6: χόρτος . . . ὡς ἄνθος χόρτου
Jas 1:10:?   ὡς ἄνθος χόρτου

Isa 40:7: ἐξηράνθη ὁ χόρτος καὶ τὸ ἄνθος ἐξέπεσεν
Jas 1:11: ἐξηράνεν τὸν χόρτον καὶ τὸ ἄνθος αὐτοῦ ἐξέπεσεν

Isa 40:9: ὑψηλὸν . . . ὕψωσον . . . ὑψώσατε
Jas 1:9: ὕψει

When one keeps in mind that the first part of Isaiah 40 was a popular passage for the early church (it is often quoted and alluded to in the New Testament) and that it appears to have been also quite important for various groups within Judaism, we may infer that it was a very well known portion of the Bible and further that the observed parallels constituted an allusion for the first audience: the informed hearers of James were probably reminded of Isaiah 40.

Now how does this help us with the interpretation of James 1, and what do the Dead Sea Scrolls have to contribute? There are at least three questions regarding Jas 1:9–11 that interpreters debate. First, who are the wicked here? Are they rich Christians or are they rich outsiders without any hope? Second, is our passage about the fate that the rich will suffer in this life or are we rather to think about the last judgment? Third, the words translated by the NRSV as "the sun rises with its scorching heat" can also be rendered, "the sun rises with the scorching wind." Which rendering is correct?

One particular passage in the Scrolls helps us with each of these questions. That passage is column 1 of *4QSapiential Work (4Q185)*. Lines 7–13 are as follows:

> And who can endure in front of his angels? For, like burning fire will he judge [. . .] of his spirits. But you, O sons of man, woe to you! For see, he sprouts like grass and his loveliness blooms like a flower. His grace makes the wind blow over him and his root

shrivels, and his leaves: the wind scatters them, until hardly anything remains in his place, and nothing but wind is found.

This, like Jas 1:9–11, is allusive and clearly takes up the language of Isa 40:6–7. Furthermore, we should note that in doing so it speaks not of the heat of the sun but of the dryness caused by the desert wind. Now most commentators have assumed that James's phrase about the sun implies that the following words must mean something like "with (its) scorching heat." But others have argued that the Greek means rather "with scorching wind." They seem to be correct. For not only is the latter the most common meaning of the Greek in the Septuagint, but the wind also causes the flowers of the field to perish in Ps 103:15–16, and Jonah 4:8 connects the rising of the sun with the coming of the east wind ("And it happened at the rising of the sun that God directed a burning wind . . ."). When one adds further that just such a connection lies behind the Arabic word *sharq*, that is, "sirocco," whose etymological meaning is, according to the dictionaries, "the rising of the sun, the east," the case seems to be made. It is now strengthened by *4QSapiental Work*, which shows us that Isa 40:6–7 was associated with the powers of the desert wind.

What about the question of when the wicked can be expected to lose their riches? Some commentaries apply the words to the here and now. Others—now the majority—think of eschatological judgment. The former have on their side the text of Isaiah itself, which is definitely not about the final judgment, as well as passages such as 1 Sam 2:4–5 ("The bows of the mighty are broken, but the feeble gird on strength. Those who were full have hired themselves out for bread, but those who were hungry are fat with spoil") and Prov 29:23 ("A person's pride will bring humiliation, but one who is lowly in spirit will obtain honor"). In these texts, fortunes are reversed already in this life. *4QSapiential Work*, however, now shows us that Isa 40:6–7 was already turned into an eschatological text sometime before James, and this greatly strengthens the view of those who have argued that Jas 1:9–11 has the same general import as the saying of Jesus in Matthew 20:16—the last will be first and the first will be last.

On this reading, James, like Jesus, is not offering an implausible generalization about present experience. He rather knows the sad truth to be that in this world all too often the rich get richer and the poor get poorer. Like Luke 6:20 and 24, which bless the poor and censure the rich, James instead says that those on top will not be on top forever, and that those on the bottom will not always be on the bottom: the eschatological reversal wrought by God will set things right.

This reading is also consistent with the future tenses that James uses: "will pass away," "will fade away." What is envisaged is the final judgment, in anticipation of which the lowly may even now rejoice.

But what then about the identity of the wicked who are characterized by James's use of Isa 40:6–7 (the grass withers and the flower falls)? Both the Hebrew Bible and the Septuagint apply the imagery to human beings in general. The *Targum*, however, thinks of the wicked in particular: "[6] All the wicked are as the grass, and all their strength like the chaff of the field. [7] The grass withers, its flower fades, for the spirit from the Lord blows upon it; surely the wicked among the people are reckoned as the grass. [8] The wicked dies, his conceptions perish; but the word of our God abides for ever."

We unfortunately do not know the date when the targum on Isaiah was composed. But that here it contains old tradition is confirmed by 2 *Bar.* 82:7, a late first-century source which likewise applies the imagery of Isa 40:6–7 to the wicked: "And we think about the beauty of their gracefulness while they go down in impurities; but like grass which is withering, they will fade away."

What does *4QSapiential Work* have to contribute on this score? Unlike the targum and 2 *Bar.* 82:7, it does not apply the words of Isa 40:6–7 solely to the wicked. On the other hand, it is not addressing humanity in general. *4QSapiential Work* rather has the people of Israel in general within its focus. It admittedly begins with the universal address, "But you, O sons of man, woe to you." But the use of Isa 40:6–7 is followed by this: "And now, please, hear me, my people! Simpletons, pay attention to me . . . Why do you give your soul to futility . . . Listen to me, my sons, and do not defy the words of YHWH."

These words are not addressed to the members of the Qumran Community in particular but rather to the chosen people of God in general. So *4QSapiential Work* attests to a reinterpretation of Isa 40:6–7, a reinterpretation that focuses the words upon Israel. This is why it speaks to those whose salvation is yet in doubt. Such are being called, through a general admonition directed to all, to take care, to abandon their futility. So whether or not outsiders ever in fact read 4QSapiential Work, it does pose as though speaking to them directly.

We appear to have the very same phenomenon in James. For James presents itself in more than one place as addressing itself to outsiders. Jas 4:1–10, for example, accuses the readers of having committed murder while 5:1–6 tells them that their clothes are moth-eaten, that the rust of their silver and gold will eat their flesh like fire, and that they have condemned and murdered "the righteous one." None of this is easy to imagine as addressed to Christians. So we need to question those who take Jas 1:1 ("To the twelve tribes in the dispersion") to refer either to Jewish Christians or to the church universal. Given the content of James, it is much more natural to take the first sentence in James to mean exactly what it says. James, that is, presents itself as a book written to Jews, whether Christian or not.

Within this view of things, Jas 1:9–11 need not be restricted to Christians; indeed, it is far more natural to think of the rich of 1:10–11, the rich who wither away at the eschatological judgment, as outsiders, as people who do not belong to the community, as the same group condemned in chapters 4 and 5. And in this case the parallel with *4QSapiential Work* is all the greater. For although both texts were presumably read primarily or even exclusively by insiders, they present themselves as addressed to outsiders. In other words, both James and *4QSapiential Work* take up the language of Isa 40:6–7 against its original sense and universal scope and narrow it so that it is reapplied to warn outsiders of the fate that will befall the wicked.

The Anointed Herald of Isaiah 61 and the Beatitudes.

The first words that Jesus speaks in the Sermon on the Mount are these: "Blessed are the poor in spirit, for theirs is the kingdom of heaven. Blessed are those who mourn, for they will be comforted. Blessed are the meek, for they will inherit the earth. Blessed are those who hunger and thirst for righteousness, for they will be filled." These well-known verses allude to the beginning of Isaiah 61:

> The Spirit of the Lord is upon me, because the Lord has
> anointed me; he has sent me to bring good news to the op-
> pressed, to bind up the brokenhearted, to proclaim liberty to
> the captives, and release to the prisoners; to proclaim the year
> of the Lord's favor, and the day of vengeance to our God; to
> comfort all who mourn (verses 1–2).

Jesus is drawing upon Isaiah not just when he says that those who
mourn will be comforted: his promise to the poor is also based
upon that prophet. For the Greek translation of the Hebrew line,
"to bring good news to the oppressed," uses for "oppressed" the
same word that in Matthew is traditionally rendered "poor" (*ptōchos*).
Moreover, Isaiah's "to bring good news" is related to Jesus' promise of the kingdom, for in the Gospels it is precisely the kingdom of
God that is the subject of preaching good news.

What all of this means is that the beatitudes are not simply
exhortations to this or that virtue or promises of future reward.
They are also christological assertions. That is, the speaker of Matthew 5 is laying implicit claim to being Isaiah's herald. If there were
any doubt, it is dispelled by Matt 11:2–6 (compare Luke 7:22–23):

> When John heard in prison what the Messiah was doing, he sent
> word by his disciples and said to him, "Are you the one who is to
> come, or are we to wait for another?" Jesus answered them, "Go
> and tell John what you hear and see: the blind receive their
> sight, the lame walk, the lepers are cleansed, the deaf hear, the
> dead are raised, and the poor have good news preached to
> them. And blessed is anyone who takes no offense at me."

Jesus' answer to John consists mostly of a list of items culled from
the book of Isaiah that match Jesus' ministry. The last item is this:
"the poor have good news preached to them." The dependence
upon Isa 61:1 (Greek: *euangelisasthai ptōchois*; compare Matthew's
ptōchoi euangelizontai) is unmistakable. Jesus is saying, among other
things, I am the herald foreseen by Isaiah.

This claim has now been illumined by the Dead Sea Scrolls. In
more than one place, we find Isa 61:1–3 used to characterize
eschatological figures. In column 2 of *11QMelchizedek*, for instance,
a citation of Deut 15:2 ("And this is the manner of the remission:
every creditor shall remit the claim that is held against a neighbor
of the community, because the Lord's remission has been pro-
claimed") is followed immediately by this: "[Its inter]pretation for
the last days refers to the captives, about whom he said: 'To

proclaim liberty to the captives' (Isa 61:1). And he will make their rebels prisoners [. . .] and of the inheritance of Melchizedek, for [. . .] and they are the inheri[tance of Melchi]zedek, who will make them return. He will proclaim liberty for them, to free them from [the debt] of all their iniquities." Here Melchizedek, who in the scrolls becomes a savior of the end-time and is almost certainly to be identified with Michael the archangel, is said to proclaim liberty to the captives. In other words, here Isaiah's oracle is seemingly applied to an angelic savior who is to come and (as it says a few lines down) "carry out the vengeance of God's judges."

　　The same passage from Isaiah is drawn upon a bit later in the very same document. Towards the end of column 2 there is this:

> How beautiful upon the mountains are the feet of the messenger who announces peace, of the mess[enger of good who announces salvation,] saying to Zion: 'your God [reigns."] Its interpretation: The mountains are the pro[phets . . .] And the messenger is [the ano]inted of the spirit about whom Dan[iel] spoke [. . . and the messenger of] good who announces salv[ation is the one about whom it is written that [he will send him "to comfo[rt the afflicted, to watch over the afflicted ones of Zion" (Isa 61:2–3).] "To comfo[rt the afflicted," its interpretation:] to instruct them in all the ages of the worl[d . . .] in truth.

These words speak of a messenger who will fulfill Isaiah's prophecy. Whether he is to be identified with Melchizedek or is a forerunner of Melchizedek is unclear. But what *11QMelchizedek* does not leave in doubt is that the beginning of Isaiah 61 was understood by the members of the sect not as a text about the past but as a text about the future; and they read it to say that, in the end-time, there would come one or more eschatological figures who would bring good news to the oppressed, proclaim liberty to the captives, and comfort all who mourn.

　　This expectation shows up in another important Qumran text. The following words are from fragment 2 of column 2 of *4QMessianic Apocalypse (4Q521)*:

> [for the heav]ens and the earth will listen to his Messiah, [and all] that is in them will not turn away from the holy precepts. Be encouraged, you who are seeking the Lord in his service! Will you not, perhaps, encounter the Lord in it, all those who hope in their hearts? For the Lord will observe the devout, and call the just by name, and upon the poor he will place his spirit, and the faithful

he will renew with his strength. For he will honor the devout upon the throne of eternal royalty, freeing prisoners, giving sight to the blind, straightening out the twisted. Ever shall I cling to those who hope. In his mercy he will jud[ge,] and from no-one shall the fruit [of] good [deeds] be delayed, and the Lord will perform marvelous acts such as have not existed, just as he sa[id] for he will heal the badly wounded, and will make the dead live, he will proclaim good news to the meek, give lavishly [to the need], lead the exiled and enrich the hungry. [. . .] and all [. . .]

For several reasons this text, which we have already looked at in chapter 2, is of exceptional interest for students of the New Testament. Here I should like to focus on the fact that once more we find a phrase from Isaiah 61 in a description of what is to happen in the latter days: "proclaim good news to the meek" is from Isa 61:1.

Strangely enough, however, the subject of the verb "proclaim" is the Lord. That is, grammatically God will proclaim good news to the meek. But nowhere in the Hebrew Bible is God the subject of that verb (בשׂר); and in *11QMelchizedek* the eschatological herald or heralds are instruments of God, not the divinity. So one must suspect that this is also the case here: the work of the divine representative is such that God can be spoken of as the subject. That is, God, through an eschatological representative, "his Messiah," will free prisoners, give sight to the blind, straighten out the twisted, perform marvelous acts, heal the badly wounded, make the dead live, and proclaim good news to the meek.

Given the fragmentary nature of *4Q521*, we cannot be sure exactly what figure is designated by the term, "his Messiah," literally "his anointed one." It might be the Davidic Messiah. In the New Testament, Jesus is the Davidic Messiah and also the herald of Isaiah 61. Or it might be a prophet like Elijah. One recalls the New Testament's identification of John the Baptist with Elijah according to Mal 4:5 ("Lo, I will send you the prophet Elijah before the great and terrible day of the Lord"). Or it might be still some other figure of the end-time. For the Scrolls look forward to several additional figures, including a priestly Messiah, Melchizedek, and a prophet like Moses. Beyond that, given that eschatological expectations are often vague because the future always remains dim, despite our hopes, perhaps we should not persist is trying to be more specific. Maybe the author of *4Q451* did not have a clear idea as to the relationship between the herald of Isaiah 61 and other eschatological figures.

Even if we cannot solve this problem, the use of Isaiah 61 in *4Q521* holds at least two lessons for interpreters of the New Testament. First, the fragment is additional evidence that some pre-Christian Jews saw in Isaiah 61 a picture of eschatological prophecies that would come to pass in their near future. So when followers of Jesus saw in him a figure who could be characterized by the language of Isa 61:1–3, they were not calling attention for the first time to a neglected text but rather claiming the fulfillment of a well-known expectation.

Second, the line from Isaiah 61 in *4Q521* is part of a list of expectations. They include:

➤ giving sight to the blind
➤ straightening out the twisted
➤ performing marvelous acts
➤ healing the badly wounded
➤ making the dead live

These items seem to be drawn in part from other parts of Isaiah (see for instance 26:19; 29:18; 35:5–6; 42:7, 18). Now it is striking that a very similar list, also largely constructed out of lines from Isaiah, appears in Matt 11:2–6 and Luke 7:22–23 leading up to "the poor have good news preached to them":

➤ the blind see again
➤ the lame walk
➤ the lepers are cleansed
➤ the deaf hear
➤ the dead are raised

The two similar lists do not demand literary dependence. But they do probably tell us that Isa 61:1 was commonly brought into connection with other lines from Isaiah in order to create a picture of the eschatological future. In the New Testament Jesus' ministry brings that picture to realization. In *4Q521* that picture has not yet been realized. The reason takes us to the final chapter of this book.

The End in Zechariah and the End of Jesus

I n Mark 11 we read that, when Jesus and his disciples were approaching Jerusalem, he directed two of them with the following words: "Go into the village ahead of you, and immediately as you enter it, you will find tied there a colt that has never been ridden; untie it and bring it. If anyone says to you, 'Why are you doing this? just say this, 'The Lord needs it and will send it back here immediately'" (verses 1–3). This is a story with many strange features. I should like, however, to focus here only on a detail that most English readers of the text undoubtedly pass over without thought. Mark describes the colt as "tied." This is the sort of specific detail one should pause to consider because details like it are so rare in the gospels. In a narrative so otherwise sparse, why bother with such a superfluous comment?

Commentators, beginning already in the second century, have regularly found here an allusion to a Hebrew Bible text (see for example Justin Martyr's *First Apology* 32:6 and Clement of Alexandria's *The Instructor* 1:5:15). In Gen 49:10–11, Jacob prophesies that "the scepter shall not depart from Judah, nor the ruler's staff from between his feet, until tribute comes to him; and the obedience of the peoples is his. Binding his foal to the vine and his donkey's colt to the choice vine, he washes his garments in wine and his robe in the blood of grapes . . ." This line was given a messianic interpretation in Judaism. In *Targum Onqelos*, for example, Gen 49:10 is paraphrased thus: "The ruler shall never depart from the House of Judah, nor the scribe from his children's children for evermore—until the Messiah comes, whose is the kingdom, and him shall the nations obey."

The Dead Sea Scrolls also attest to this understanding of Gen 49:10–11. Column 5 of *4QGenesis Pesher*[a] contains the following: "A sovereign shall [not] be removed from the tribe of Judah. While Israel has the dominion, there will [not] lack someone who sits on the throne of David. For 'the staff' is the covenant of royalty, [the thou]sands of Israel are 'the feet.' Until the messiah of justice comes, the branch of David. For to him and to his descendants has been given the covenant of royalty over his people for all everlasting generations . . ." These words guarantee that the messianic interpretation of Genesis 49:10–11 found in the targum goes back to pre-Christian times and so greatly strengthens the idea of an allusion to that text in Mark 11:1–3.

Mark, however, appears to be alluding to a second Hebrew Bible text at the same time. For his comment that the donkey is one upon which no one has ever sat echoes not Genesis 49 but rather the Greek version of the messianic prophecy in Zech 9:9, which has this: "Behold, the king is coming to you, just and a savior. He is meek and riding on an ass, and a young foal." Here the donkey of the coming king is "young" or "new." This corresponds to Jesus' donkey, which has not yet been ridden.

The plausibility that Mark has in mind the text from Zechariah as well as that from Genesis (so already Justin and Clement of Alexandria) is enhanced by three facts . The first is that the Hebrew of Zech 9:9 (*ben-ʾătōnô*, "donkey's colt") may itself very well be designed to recall Gen 49:11 (*běnî-ʾătōnô*, "his donkey's colt"). That is, the Hebrew Bible may here already allude to itself so that one thinking about Gen 49:11 might also recall Zech 9:9.

The second fact is that rabbinic sources bring the two texts together (*Gen. Rab.* on 32:6 and on 49:11, for instance).

The third fact is that Matthew not only, like Mark, alludes to Gen 49:10–11 by mentioning that the colt is tied, but he, like John (12:15), actually cites Zech 9:9: "This took place to fulfill what had been spoken through the prophet, saying, 'Tell the daughter of Zion, Look, your king is coming to you, humble, and mounted on a donkey, and on a colt, the foal of a donkey.'" So here we find explicit what remains only implicit in Mark: Jesus' entry into Jerusalem fulfills the prophecy of Zech 9:9.

At this point I should like to observe that Zech 9:9 is only one of a several verses from the latter half of Zechariah that are alluded to or quoted in the canonical passion narratives. One can see this from the following table:

Quotation	Allusion
From Mark	
11:1–3	Zech 9:9
11:15–19	Zech 14:16, 20–21
14:11	Zech 11:12
14:22–25	Zech 9:11
14:26–31	Zech 13:7
14:50–51	Zech 13:7(?); 14:5(?)
From Matthew add:	
21:4–5	Zech 9:9
26:15	Zech 11:12
27:3–10	Zech 11:12–13
27:51–53	Zech 4:4–5
From John add:	
12:15	Zech 9:9
19:37	Zech 12:10

Along with the Psalms and Isaiah 40–55, Zechariah 9–14 was clearly one of those portions of Scripture to which early Christians turned when they contemplated the passion of Jesus. Now the impetus for drawing upon the Psalms and Isaiah 40–55 is pretty obvious. These texts often have to do with the sufferings of the saints, or even with the suffering of a particular righteous individual. Further, Psalms 22, 41, 69, 71, and Isaiah 53 foretell the vindication or exaltation of the righteous one who suffers. So application of these passages to Jesus is altogether natural. But what does one make of the latter half of Zechariah? It has a completely different character. It is in fact an apocalypse, a collection of prophecies about the latter days. It concerns the eschatological judgment and all that will accompany it. But that judgment, obviously, has not come, so why would early Christians use Zechariah's Apocalypse to interpret the passion of Jesus?

Consider Mark 14:26–31 in particular. Here we find a quotation from Zech 13:7: "I will strike the shepherd, and the sheep will be scattered." This is designed to interpret Jesus' prediction in

Mark 14:27a, "You will all fall away." The verse quoted, Zech 13:7, belongs to a larger passage of Scripture, Zech 13:7 – 14:5, that is primarily a prophecy of the tribulations that are to precede the great and terrible Day of the Lord. The verse in fact heads the section. One may accordingly ask whether, within its present Markan context, one of its chief functions is not to recall all of Zech 13:7 – 14:5, so that the reader comes to think that the hour of desolation and testing foretold by Zechariah has come to pass, or rather begun to come to pass, with the striking of the shepherd (= Jesus) and the scattering of his flock (= the disciples).

Of course, on the assumption that "atomistic exegesis" of the Hebrew Bible was then the rule (that is, that people typically heard quotations without paying attention to their original scriptural contexts) it is nowadays fashionable to prohibit taking account of the original contexts of Scriptures cited in the New Testament. But such an evaluation of first-century hermeneutics is not entirely satisfactory. And in the present case in particular, that Zech 13:7 would at least make one think about the end of the ages is manifest from copy B from the Genizah of the *Damascus Document* (only fragmentary portions of which have survived in Qumran caves 4 and 6). Column 19 contains the following:

> But (over) all those who despise the precepts and the ordinances, may be emptied over them the punishment of the wicked, when God visits the earth, when there comes the word which is written by the hand of Zechariah, the prophet: "Wake up, sword, against my shepherd, and against the male who is my companion—oracle of God—wound the shepherd and scatter the flock and I shall return my hand upon the little ones." Those who are faithful to him are the poor ones of the flock. These shall escape in the age of visitation; but those that remain shall be delivered up to the sword when there comes the messiah of Aaron and Israel (5–11).

Here the citation of Zech 13:7 is cited when the author is describing the horrible punishments that will accompany the eschatological judgment, when the Messiah will return.

Once again then we must ask, how can the prophecies of Zechariah be related to the passion of Jesus? It makes sense that, at Qumran, the prophecies of Zechariah are yet to be realized, for the eschatological day of the Lord with its attendant judgment has not come. History runs its course as ever. But how then, on the other hand, could early Christians ever have seen the fulfillment of Zechariah's eschatological prophecies in history?

The question is the more pressing because Jesus' passion actually relates itself to a second apocalypse, namely, his own eschatological discourse. Mark 13, which is generally, and quite rightly, taken to be for the most part a prophecy about the end of the ages, about the visible coming of the Son of Man on the clouds of heaven and the events leading up to it, contains the following prophecies and admonitions:

> Mark 13:24: the sun will be darkened
> Mark 13:2: the temple will be destroyed
> Mark 13:35–36: "watch . . . lest the master come and find them sleeping"
> Mark 13:9: the disciples will be "delivered up"
> Mark 13:9: the disciples will appear before Jewish councils
> Mark 13:9: the disciples will be beaten
> Mark 13:9: the disciples will stand before governors and kings
> Mark 13:12–13: brother will deliver brother over to death
> Mark 13:14–16: people will flee

It is quite striking, and cannot be coincidence, that the nine items just listed are, in an odd sort of way, all paralleled in the passion narrative (Mark 14–15)—which, it should be underlined, is introduced precisely by Mark 13:

> Mark 15:33: when Jesus is crucified the sun goes dark
> Mark 15:38: the Temple is symbolically destroyed when the veil is torn
> Mark 14:34, 38: Jesus tells his disciples to "watch"; then he "comes" and "finds" them "sleeping"
> Mark 14:10, 21, 41, etc.: Jesus is "delivered up"
> Mark 14:53–65: Jesus appears before a Jewish council
> Mark 14:65: Jesus is beaten
> Mark 15:1–15: Jesus appears before Pilate the governor
> Mark 14:10, 20, 43: one of those closest to him hands Jesus over
> Mark 14:50–52: when Jesus is betrayed the disciples flee

How are we to understand all this parallelism? Evidently, and despite the ongoing course of history, the crucifixion and the events leading to it were somehow thought to have fulfilled apocalyptic expectations. So Mark's passion narrative is, so to speak, an end of the world in miniature. What will happen at the culmination has already happened, or begun to happen, in the end of Jesus. That is, the Gospels present us with a bit of what has been called "realized eschatology." Notwithstanding the fact that the New Testament still looks forward to history's culmination, it surprisingly claims that many eschatological expectations have come to pass. The explanation for this lies primarily in the Christian confession of Jesus as Messiah.

Christians now reading the messianic prophecies of the Hebrew Bible are apt to think that while one verse envisions the first advent of the Messiah, the next envisions his second advent. Christians presuppose, in the light of history, that Jesus came once and will come again. That is, they believe in two advents, Jesus' first coming and his second coming. And they find all this in the prophecies of the Hebrew Bible. But this belief in two messianic advents arose only out of the wholly unexpected circumstance that the appearance of the Messiah did not coincide with history's culmination. Although the Messiah, so Christians confessed, had come, against all expectation nature had not been transformed, Israel had not been delivered, and all sin and evil had not been defeated. Christians believed that the Messiah had appeared, and it followed for them that prophecies must have been fulfilled; but they also knew that so much that had been expected to accompany the Messiah's advent had not happened that they could not but believe many additional prophecies still awaited fulfillment. In other words, the large gap between messianic expectation and the actualities of history indicated that the Messiah's initial appearance could not have fulfilled without remainder all of the eschatological hopes supported by the Hebrew Bible. For that another advent was necessary.

This belief in two advents was not, it must be emphasized, something shared by ancient Jews. The reason is understandable. Considered objectively, the Hebrew Bible does not clearly or explicitly teach a doctrine of two messianic advents. The prophecies of the Hebrew Bible do not look forward to two great saving events but one. So it did not occur to anyone reading the Scriptures before Christianity to suppose that God's anointed would come once, then depart, and then come again.

It took even the church itself some time to see things in exactly this way. The earliest Christians, who continued to live within the Jewish tradition, still understood the Hebrew Bible to look forward to one grand event, not two. For them, then, everything associated with the Messiah was yet eschatological, that is, everything had to do with the end. They did not think of some messianic prophecies as clustered around the middle of history, others around the end of time. They did not imagine a time line with the Messiah's first advent in the center, his second advent at the end. They instead saw a time line that had ended in their own era, or was about to end. This explains why Paul and other early Christians seem to have hoped for or expected the near-end of the world as we know it (see Luke 19:11; Acts 1:6; Rom 13:11–12). It also explains why Jesus' ministry is, throughout the New Testament, construed in eschatological categories—and also why the passion narrative interprets Jesus' fate as the fulfillment of eschatological prophecies. For the earliest Christians, every fulfillment was an eschatological fulfillment. The Messiah had come, and so history was winding down. If Jesus had suffered tribulation and risen from the dead, the same things were about to happen to all the saints.

Ancient Jews, including those who wrote the Dead Sea Scrolls, still expected the Messiah to come, the dead to be raised, the judgment to fall, the devil to be routed, sin to be defeated, and the new creation to appear. For them all these things belonged to the future. For the early Christians, however, the eschatological had already been set in motion. Zechariah's prophecies of the latter days had commenced to find fulfillment. The Messiah had come (Mark 8:29: "Peter answered him, 'You are the Messiah'"). The dead had been raised (Matt 27:51–53: "the tombs were opened, and many bodies of the saints who had fallen asleep were raised"). The judgment had fallen (John 12:31: "Now is the judgment of this world"). The devil had been routed (John 13:31: "Now shall the ruler of this world be cast out"). Sin had been defeated (Rom 8:1–4: "the law of the Spirit of life in Christ Jesus has set you free from the law of sin and death . . . he condemned sin in the flesh"). And there had been a new creation (2 Cor 5:17: "If anyone is in

Christ, there is a new creation"). In short, in the life, death, and resurrection of Jesus and their aftermath, the kingdom of God had begun to come. It is this fundamental eschatological conviction that, despite all they shared in common, separated the early Jewish followers of Jesus from other Jews, and continues to separate the two faiths even to this day.

Conclusion

Allusions do not insist on their own way. They are only potentially transparent; hearers or readers must live and move and have their being in the right precursor texts. For those who live elsewhere, outside the right tradition, much can be missed. When Heb 13:2 enjoins, "Do not neglect to show hospitality to strangers, for by doing so some have entertained angels unawares," nothing is said about Abraham, so only those who know well the story in Genesis 18-19 will catch the allusion. Everything depends upon the capabilities of the audience. What is manifest to some can be nonexistent to others. When those of us who grew up in the 1950s and 1960s heard Don McLean's popular song, "American Pie," we did not need a commentator to tell us that the "sergeants" who "played a marching tune" were the Beatles in their late phase, or that "Jack Flash" had something to do with the Rolling Stones. But those without the requisite musical knowledge could only have heard nonsense.

I recently read John Buchan's novel, *Greenmantle.*[1] The explanatory notes at the end clarify the following: "left out at Pentecost," "spoiling the Egyptians," "string up like Haman," "What came you forth to seek?," "By the waters of Babylon, we sat down and wept," "Nimrod," "ephod," and "Passover Feast." But when the book was written, over eighty years ago, surely few of these expressions needed explanation: Buchan could assume a certain amount of biblical literacy among his intended public—which is

---

1 John Buchan, *Greenmantle* (Oxford/New York: Oxford University Press, 1993).

why the notes are not in the earlier editions. Today, however, biblical literacy has declined sufficiently that readers require commentary. Ours is the age of the annotated Bible, when people need a footnote in order to learn that when Jer 20:16 speaks in passing of "the cities that the Lord overthrew without pity," the oblique reference is to Sodom and Gomorrah. The lesson is that time deletes. Things that were once obvious can, as a text's audience changes, evaporate.

This is where the Dead Sea Scrolls and historians of ancient Judaism and Christianity can, as I have tried to show, help us. Recent scholarship has increasingly shown us not only that the Hebrew Bible is a collection of interacting texts but also that it is constantly alluded to in the old religious writings of Christians and Jews, including the Dead Sea Scrolls. The Scrolls in particular help us to see how many biblical texts were understood at the turn of the era and further how easily they could be conjured up with just the right word or phrase. In other words, the Scrolls drive home the lesson that the New Testament is not a linguistic island or an isolated revelation, but instead the offspring of parental texts, which it understands through the Jewish tradition and honors through consistent interaction and allusion.

Further Reading

Chapter 1: Introduction

Hays, Richard. *Echoes of Scripture in the Letters of Paul.* New Haven and London: Yale, 1991.

Marcus, Joel. *The Way of the Lord: Christological Exegesis of the Old Testament in the Gospel of Mark.* Edinburgh: T. & T. Clark, 1992.

Moessner, D. P. *The Lord of the Banquet: The Literary and Theological Significance of the Lukan Travel Narrative.* Minneapolis: Fortress, 1989.

Chapter 2: The Dove at the Baptism and Gen 1:2

Allison, Dale C., Jr. "The Baptism of Jesus and a New Dead Sea Scroll." *Biblical Archaeology Review* 18 (1992): 58–60.

Chapter 3: The New Moses of the New Exodus

Allison, Dale C., Jr. *The New Moses: A Matthean Typology.* Minneapolis: Fortress, 1993.

Chapter 4: Excommunication and Lev 19:17–18

Kugel, J. L. "On Hidden Hatred and Open Reproach: Early Exegesis of Leviticus 19:17." *Harvard Theological Review* 80 (1987): 43–61.

Chapter 5: The Trial of the Son of God and 2 Samuel 7

Betz, Otto. *What Do We Know about Jesus?* Philadelphia: Westminster, 1968.

Juel, Donald. *Messiah and Temple: The Trial of Jesus in the Gospel of Mark.* Society of Biblical Literature Dissertation. Missoula, Montana: Scholars Press, 1977.

Chapter 6: Uses of Isaiah in the Gospels and Jesus

Allison, Dale C., Jr. *The Intertextual Jesus: Scripture in Q.* Harrisburg: Trinity Press Internatinal, 2000.

Baumgarten, J. M. "4Q500 and the Ancient Conception of the Lord's Vineyard." *Journal of Jewish Studies* 40 (1989): 1–6.

Collins, John J. "The Works of the Messiah." *Dead Sea Scroll Discoveries* 1 (1993): 1–15.

Marcus, Joel. "The Intertextual Polemic of the Markan Vineyard Parable." In *Tolerance and Intolerance in Early Judaism and Christianity*, ed. Graham N. Stanton and Guy G. Stroumsa, 211–227. Cambridge: University Press, 1998.

Chapter 7: The End in Zechariah and the End of Jesus

Allison, Dale C., Jr. *The End of the Ages has Come: An Early Interpretation of the Passion and Resurrection of Jesus.* Studies on the New Testament and Its World. Edinburgh: T. & T. Clark, 1987.

About the Author

Dale Allison is Errett M. Grable Associate Professor of New Testament and Early Christianity at Pittsburgh Theological Seminary. He earned his B.A. (philosophy) from Wichita State University, and an M.A. and Ph.D. in biblical studies from Duke University. He has taught at the University of Glasgow, Friends University, Kansas Newman College, Wichita State University, and Saint Paul School of Theology. He has published numerous articles and several books, most recently *Jesus of Nazareth: Millenarian Prophet* (Fortress, 1998,) *The Sermon on the Mount: Inspiring the Moral Imagination* (Crossroad, 1999), and *The Intertextual Jesus: Scripture in Q* (Trinity Press International, 2000). He is currently on the editorial board of the *Journal of Biblical Literature*.